100%

INFORMATION LITERACY SUCCESS

100%

INFORMATION LITERACY SUCCESS

FOURTH EDITION

JEFF **TUNNEY**, MBA

GWENN **WILSON**, MA

DR. BARBARA **CALABRO**, PhD
Contributing Editor

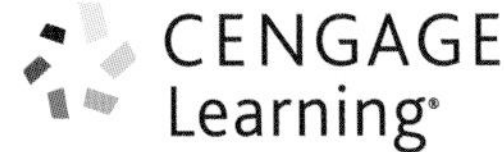

Australia • Brazil • Mexico • Singapore • United Kingdom • United States

100% Information Literacy Success
Fourth Edition
Jeff Tunney, Gwenn Wilson

Product Director: Lauren Murphy

Product Manager: Sarah Seymour

Content Developer: Courtney Triola

Product Assistant: Chip Moreland

Content Project Manager: Margaret Park Bridges

Art Director: Heather Marshall, Lumina Datamatics, Ltd.

Manufacturing Planner: Bev Breslin

IP Analyst: Ann Hoffman

IP Project Manager: Carly Belcher

Production Service: Lumina Datamatics, Ltd.

Compositor: Lumina Datamatics, Ltd.

Text and Cover Designer: Lumina Datamatics, Ltd.

Cover Image: iStockphoto.com/xijian

Library of Congress Control Number: 2016944573

ISBN: 978-1-337-10217-9

Cengage Learning
20 Channel Center Street
Boston, MA 02210
USA

Cengage Learning is a leading provider of customized learning solutions with employees residing in nearly 40 different countries and sales in more than 125 countries around the world. Find your local representative at **www.cengage.com.**

Cengage Learning products are represented in Canada by Nelson Education, Ltd.

To learn more about Cengage Learning Solutions, visit **www.cengage.com.**

Purchase any of our products at your local college store or at our preferred online store **www.cengagebrain.com.**

Printed in China
Print Number: 02 Print Year: 2017

Table of Contents

EVALUATING INFORMATION 101

LEGAL AND ETHICAL ISSUES RELATED TO INFORMATION. . .177

About the Author

JEFF TUNNEY, MBA Jeff Tunney has been an educational professional for over 12 years and has worked in computer training, continuing education, and higher educational settings. His experience in higher education consists of having served as a director of distance learning, an online course and curriculum designer, and a residential and online faculty member at the undergraduate level. Mr. Tunney has also been employed in several other professional fields, such as computer network administration, property management and development, and financial services.

Mr. Tunney earned a Master of Business Administration degree from Bentley University as well as an undergraduate degree in Finance from the University of Massachusetts. He has also had many positive experiences abroad as a student in the commerce program at the University of Wollongong in New South Wales, Australia, and as a derivatives specialist for a London-based investment company.

GWENN WILSON, MA Gwenn Wilson is a senior instructional designer with over 20 years of experience in Instructional Systems Design (ISD). She is a published author of many faculty guides, student guides, training CD-ROMs, customized curriculum for career colleges, and textbooks. As an outside consultant, Ms. Wilson has provided training and instruction for many Fortune 500 companies in areas such as sales training, leadership training, call center training, and technical training.

DR. BARBARA CALABRO, PhD, Contributing Editor Dr. Barbara Calabro is a lifelong educator. She is President of Palmetto Education Group and has held positions of Chief Academic Officer, Vice President for Academics and Vice President of Educational Support Services at the college level. Her responsibilities included institutional effectiveness, academic compliance, curriculum review and development, assessment, competency based curriculum and assessment, and professional development. In the K-12 setting, Dr. Calabro has served as a teacher, Reading consultant, principal and Curriculum Director. She is responsible for improving retention at Southwest Florida College by 3% per quarter and over 50% on a cohort basis, and is currently serving on the Board of the Foundation for Lee County Public Schools in Florida and the Consortium of Florida Education Foundations.

Preface

HOW WILL THIS TEXT HELP YOU?

Your enrollment in college says that you have made a decision to grow and develop as a person and a professional. Your college experience and your future professional activities will require you to locate, evaluate, organize, and communicate information in carrying out your responsibilities and achieving your professional goals. *100% Information Literacy Success* will provide you with tools to accomplish your objectives.

100% Information Literacy Success discusses skills that are fundamental to becoming an information-literate student and professional, which in turn will contribute to your academic and career success. The text is divided into the following topics: *Introduction to Information Literacy*, *Determining the Information You Need*, *How Do You Find and Access Information*, *Evaluating Information*, *Organizing Information*, and concluding with *Legal and Ethical Issues Related to Information.* Use the following summaries of these sections to get an overview of the book and to determine how each topic supports you in the development of information literacy skills.

- **DEFINING INFORMATION:** You will be introduced to the concept of information literacy and why it is important to academic and career success. The abundance and rapid flow of data in the information age requires understanding, finding, using, evaluating, and communicating information effectively and efficiently.
- **UNDERSTANDING INFORMATION SOURCES:** You will gain a familiarity with commonly used as well as lesser known information sources, many of which are available in libraries and online.

- **FINDING INFORMATION SOURCES:** You will learn how to locate and access information from a variety of sources so that you can effectively solve problems and answer questions at school or in the workplace.
- **EVALUATING INFORMATION:** You will learn how to evaluate the credibility and appropriateness of web-based information sources. In addition, you will become proficient in assessing an author's expertise, as well as the currency and relevancy of print and other sources.
- **ORGANIZING INFORMATION:** As a professional, you will be required to organize your research materials in a logical manner, so that your information needs are met and the information can be easily communicated to others. Effectively organized information will enable you to accomplish your communication goals.
- **COMMUNICATING INFORMATION:** You will explore the many ways in which students and professionals share information with others. You will become familiar with channels of communication and guidelines for effective communication in the workplace. In addition to the ethical use of information, emphasis is placed on legal concerns, such as how the use of someone's intellectual property should be acknowledged.

The Fourth Edition of *100% Information Literacy Success* has been revised to actively help you develop skills beyond the classroom, focusing on those strategies necessary for 21st-century learners and workers.

HOW TO USE THIS BOOK

100% Information Literacy Success is designed to actively involve you in developing information literacy skills. The text includes the following features that will guide you through the material and provide opportunities for you to practice what you've learned.

- **LEARNING OBJECTIVES.** Learning objectives, like those listed on course syllabi, are provided to outline what you should be learning from the chapter and guide you through its main concepts. Use these objectives to identify important points, understand what you are supposed to learn, measure what you have mastered, and pinpoint areas for improvement. You are encouraged to expand your knowledge beyond the learning objectives according to your own goals and interests.

- **BE IN THE KNOW.** This feature provides vignettes on real-world situations as they relate to the chapter content. The intent of this feature is to help you focus on the subject at hand, and how you can learn from the examples provided in these content areas.
- **CASE IN POINT.** In each chapter, a case study demonstrates the application of pertinent concepts in the real world. Use the questions following each case study to stimulate your critical thinking and analytical skills. Discuss the questions with classmates. You are encouraged to think of your own application of ideas and to raise additional questions.
- **SELF-ASSESSMENT QUESTIONS.** The self-assessment questions ask you to evaluate your personal development. They are intended to increase your self-awareness and ability to understand your decisions and actions.
- **CRITICAL THINKING QUESTIONS.** The critical thinking questions challenge you to examine ideas and thoughtfully apply concepts presented in the text. These questions encourage the development of thinking skills that are crucial for efficient performance in school and in the workplace.
- **APPLY IT!.** At the end of each chapter are activities that will help you apply the concepts discussed in practical situations. Your instructor may assign these activities as part of the course requirements. Or, if they are not formally assigned, you will want to complete them for your own development.
- **SUCCESS STEPS.** Scattered throughout the text are success steps that offer a pathway to achieve various goals. They essentially summarize the detailed processes that are discussed fully in the body of the text. To achieve a specific information literacy

goal, use the Table of Contents and Index to locate the information quickly.

- **SUGGESTED ITEMS FOR LEARNING PORTFOLIO.** A portfolio is a collection of the work that you have completed. A *learning portfolio* is used to track your progress through school, and a *developmental portfolio* typically contains documents that illustrate your development over time. A professional portfolio, on the other hand, showcases your professional accomplishments and contains finished projects and work that represents your best efforts and achievements. It will be the emphasis of the portfolio you create as part of *100% Information Literacy Success.* Throughout the book, there are suggestions to include completed activities in your portfolio. Arranging your portfolio in a way that illustrates your professional development and showcases your best work will be useful for reviewing your progress and demonstrating your abilities.

As you read and complete the activities in *100% Information Literacy Success*, keep your long-term goals in mind and think about how you can apply these concepts to your everyday activities. Application is the key—and the more you practice, the more proficient you will become in using and communicating information.

TEACHING WITH 100% INFORMATION LITERACY SUCCESS

WHAT IS NEW IN THE FOURTH EDITION OF *100% INFORMATION LITERACY SUCCESS?*

Instructors who have previously used *100% Information Literacy Success* in their classrooms will find the following changes throughout the text:

- Many of the objectives and exercises have been rewritten to address the reader using a second person point of view.
- All references to chapter numbers have been replaced with chapter names.

The following list includes changes by chapter to assist instructors in transitioning to the Fourth Edition of *100% Information Literacy Success:*

CHAPTER 1:

- The section Information Literacy in the Digital Age: An Overview has been renamed Information Literacy: An Overview, and describes the topics of information work and information workers.
- The section Defining Digital Information Literacy has been renamed Defining Digital Literacy. It provides a definition of digital literacy and describes the skills and attributes of digitally literate people.
- The section Components of Information Literacy in the Digital Age has been renamed Components of Information Literacy and describes the information-related tasks an information-literate individual should be able to complete.
- Information about factors that should be considered when purchasing a computer or mobile device has been added to the Computer Literacy section.

CHAPTER 2:

- The section Primary and Secondary Information Sources has been renamed Primary and Secondary Sources and introduces the reader to the research process.
- Examples of web portals that are used in specific fields of study have been added to the Web Portals section.
- A new section, Smartphone Apps, has been added.

CHAPTER 3:

- The topic of infographics has been added to the Graphics and Images section.
- Types of Electronic Resources have expanded information on wikis, graphics and images, and social media.

- The Podcasting section has been renamed Podcasts.
- A new section, Deep Web and Dark Web, was added to the chapter.
- Additional tips on using Boolean Operators have been added.

CHAPTER 4:

- The topic of social media was added to the Author section.

CHAPTER 5:

- The section Types of Graphics was removed and its content was added to the Organizing Graphics section.
- The LibreOffice Impress suite and Google Slides app were added as topics in the Other Presentation Software section.

CHAPTER 6:

- The MLA Style section has been updated to reflect changes made in the latest edition of the MLA Handbook.
- The Information and Privacy Issues section has been updated to include right to be forgotten laws.
- The section on What Employers Seeks has been updated to tie material that students learned earlier in the book to the attributes and skills employers' desire.

ANCILLARY MATERIALS

An Instructor's Companion Site includes an Instructor's Manual, PowerPoint Slides, and more. The instructor's resources can be accessed at login.cengage.com.

You can also package this textbook with the College Success Planner to assist students in making the best use of their time both on and off campus.

For more in-depth information on any of these items, talk with your sales rep, or visit www.cengagebrain.com.

CHAPTER OUTLINE

Information Literacy: An Overview

Why Is Information Literacy Important?

Defining Digital Literacy

Components of Information Literacy

Steps in Effective Research

E+/Getty Images

Introduction to Information Literacy

LEARNING OBJECTIVES

By the end of this chapter, you will be able to:

- Describe information work and information workers.
- Define *information literacy*.
- List the specific skills required for an individual to be an information-literate student or professional.
- Explain the importance of knowing how to locate, access, retrieve, evaluate, use, and communicate information effectively in school and in the workplace.
- Explain the challenges facing an individual who does not possess information skills in school and in the workplace.

1

BE IN THE KNOW

Information Literacy and Professionalism

While you are in school, one of the smartest things you can do is groom yourself for becoming a professional in the workplace. Professionalism is defined as showing behaviors that meet the standards and expectations of the workplace. Demonstrating professionalism in both the classroom and at your place of employment is paramount to your success.

One of the ways you can demonstrate professionalism is to become an information-literate student or worker. Information-literate people can effectively find, evaluate, and communicate credible and meaningful information that is used to solve problems. When interviewing and recruiting recent graduates, employers seek out those who exhibit excellent computer skills (such as being able to conduct online research). They also place great value on graduates who go beyond the first two or three entries from a search engine to get answers that solve information problems. This means finding and evaluating information from myriad sources, and in the workplace, this often means seeking out coworkers, supervisors, or other trusted sources. As you complete your coursework, think about those people beyond your instructors who can help you with your information needs, such as librarians and professionals in your field of study. The ability to critically assess the information you find and correlate it back to the subject at hand is a skill that will help you both in your studies and in the workplace.

It is not too early to start down the path to professionalism. Exhibiting professionalism using your information literacy skills while you are in school and on the job should become a daily habit. Strive to demonstrate those skills and professionalism in everything that you do as a student and in your work position. Your diligence will pay off as you move forward in your career.

INFORMATION LITERACY: AN OVERVIEW

Due to the enormous amount of quickly changing information, students and professionals alike must be able to find reliable and relevant information and put it to use effectively. Students like you must be able to access information beyond textbooks and classroom instructors to prepare for the workplace. Professionals must keep current and continuously expand their body of knowledge to be successful and to advance in their careers. Staying up-to-date requires individuals to become *information workers* who are *information-literate.*

INFORMATION WORK AND INFORMATION WORKERS

If you use a computer, a smartphone, mobile apps, social media, cloud computing, the Internet, and email while you are in school, regardless of your field of study, you are doing *information work* and can be considered an *information worker.* Your "job" while attending classes is to seek out, analyze, and disseminate information on a particular topic or area in the form of papers, projects, and presentations. The information work that you complete while you are in school contributes to your own learning goals.

The same is said to be true for those who enter the workforce in most instances. Daniel Rasmus (2012, p. 1), a strategist and industry analyst, defines an information worker as "a person who uses information to assist in making decisions or taking actions, or a person who creates information that informs the decisions or actions of others." These days, finding, evaluating, organizing, and communicating information in a meaningful way to your company are fundamental components of most jobs, no matter your job title or position on the organizational chart. Corporations harness useful information to achieve organizational goals, such as increasing their bottom line and maintaining a competitive edge, among other things.

Infogineering.net (n.d.) identifies eight must-have skills in order to be a successful information worker, which include the ability to:

- Search online for the information you need.
- Determine if the retrieved information is accurate and reliable.
- Communicate the found information to others through the best communication channel(s).
- Use computers and operating systems.
- Use word processing, spreadsheets, and presentation software to collect and disseminate information.
- Put information into the proper file format (such as .jpg for photos) and know how to back up files.
- Perform computer security, including technical security (protecting against viruses and using security software such as firewalls), and information security (access to personal information, sending confidential information, etc.).
- Focus your attention on finding the information you need in the most efficient manner possible.

All of these "must-haves," as well as many other skills, comprise what is known as *information literacy*. The remainder of this text focuses on the components of information literacy and the importance of mastering these abilities in order to become a proficient and professional information worker.

WHAT IS INFORMATION LITERACY?

Wesleyan University (2016) describes information literacy as "a crucial skill in the pursuit of knowledge. It involves recognizing when information is needed and being able to efficiently locate, accurately evaluate, effectively use, and clearly communicate information in various formats." Today, information comes to us from a myriad of sources: the Internet, podcasts, blogs, social media, and traditional media, to name just a few. Excellent students will pursue the development of these skills and practice them in each course they take. They will apply the concepts specifically to their field of study and career goals. Information-literate individuals are also able to critically assess information and use it effectively to solve personal and workplace problems.

WHY IS INFORMATION LITERACY IMPORTANT?

Homes, schools, libraries, and workplaces have become increasingly reliant upon advanced technology, including powerful computers, higher-speed Internet connections, sophisticated software applications, convenient searching tools, and numerous media devices such as digital cameras, scanners, and wireless devices. We know that the technology is available, but do we know how to harness this technology to solve our problems and answer our questions? What do we do when we are faced with so much information? How will we know that what we find is credible? How will we communicate this information to everyone who needs to know? How do we even know what questions to ask to begin to solve our information problems?

Without advanced knowledge and skills, students and professionals alike are at a significant disadvantage in their work environments. Problems facing individuals who lack information skills include:

- asking the wrong questions (and consequently getting the wrong answers!)
- using limited or inappropriate sources of information
- using inaccurate or misleading information
- accessing outdated information
- finding incomplete information
- using biased or one-sided resources

- being inefficient in research and wasting time
- being disorganized
- communicating the information ineffectively

We cannot just be excellent learners. We must be lifelong learners to keep pace with advancing technology and new information. A college graduate's first job represents only the first step. Career advancement requires continuous development of knowledge and skills, as well as the ability and willingness to adapt quickly to the constantly changing tools of the industry. Career advancement in today's information world requires well-developed information skills. Lifelong learning requires taking the initiative to continue to learn and also to figure out what you need to learn.

Self-Assessment Questions

- Think carefully about your career field or a field in which you might be interested. What technologies do you predict for this field in the next 10 years? How do you see a job in this field changing because of these technologies? Write down as many different ideas as you can.
- How might you prepare yourself for continued success and career advancement in a specific field? What about the workplace in general?

1

ADVANTAGES OF BEING INFORMATION-LITERATE

When you become information-literate, you increase your advantages in school and in the workplace. The following list represents just a few of these potential advantages:

- You sharpen your critical and creative thinking skills.
- You develop higher-order thinking skills essential for excellence in school and the workplace.
- You develop a deeper and more applicable understanding of the content you are learning in school, and therefore become better prepared for your jobs.
- You are able to communicate in knowledgeable, logical, and defensible ways regarding your work.
- Your ability to effectively participate in problem solving and decision making is enhanced.
- You are able to keep up with advancements in your field of study, making you more competent and valuable as employees.

DEFINING DIGITAL LITERACY

As we move further into the 21st century, we find that how information literacy is defined takes on additional significance. According to Jones and Flannigan (n.d. p. 5), professors and researchers for the National Association for Community College Entrepreneurship (NACCE),

1

> "*Digital literacy* represents a person's ability to perform tasks effectively in a digital environment. The term *digital* means information represented in numeric form and primarily for use by a computer. The term *literacy* includes the ability to read and interpret media (text, sound, images, etc.), to reproduce data and images through digital manipulation, and to evaluate and apply new knowledge gained from digital environments."

The American Library Association Digital Literacy Task Force (2013, p. 2) defines digital literacy as "the ability to use information and communication technologies to find, understand, evaluate, create, and communicate digital information, an ability that requires both cognitive and technical skills."

The Association defines a *digitally literate person* as one who:

- "possesses the variety of skills—cognitive and technical—required to find, understand, evaluate, create, and communicate digital information in a wide variety of formats;
- is able to use diverse technologies appropriately and effectively to search for and retrieve information, interpret search results, and judge the quality of the information retrieved;
- understands the relationships among technology, lifelong learning, personal privacy, and appropriate stewardship of information;
- uses these skills and the appropriate technologies to communicate and collaborate with peers, colleagues, family, and on occasion the general public;
- uses these skills to participate actively in civic society and contribute to a vibrant, informed, and engaged community" (ALA, Digital Literacy Task Force 2013, p. 2).

Today, the information-literate learner must combine the knowledge of how to find, evaluate, and communicate information within the context of a digitized environment.

COMPONENTS OF INFORMATION LITERACY

To execute information-related tasks effectively, students and professionals must develop an efficient information-gathering process and enhance specific information-related skills. The ALA (2000) has published information literacy standards for students in higher education. Although technology and information sources have expanded significantly since publications of these standards, the standards are not medium-specific, which makes their concepts applicable today. According to the ALA Standards, an information-literate individual should be able to complete the following information-related tasks:

- **DEFINE:** *Define the need, problem, or question.*

  For example, a small training company wants to start offering its training workshops to customers in another state. To do so legally, efficiently, and wisely, the company first must answer several questions about the new area: (1) Does the new state have any laws or regulations for this type of business? (2) Does the new area have competition that would make the decision to expand unwise? (3) Does the new area have enough potential customers—those who would be interested in the type of training the company offers—to make the training cost-effective?

- **FIND:** *Locate, access, and retrieve the information from a variety of print, electronic, and human information sources.*

  In the example, the company must find the information to answer the questions about expansion into the new state. The training manager responsible for the expansion must understand the specific resources that are available and that will provide her with the correct and current information. She then must be able to locate the resources and access the information. Understanding current search techniques and tools will be necessary for the training manager to access the most current information.

  Once she has accessed the information, she must be able to retrieve it so she can organize it and present it to the company president later. The needed information might include state and local regulations, market reports, and demographic information. Sources might include state and local governments, market surveys, directories, and other data services. From numerous resources, the training manager must select the information that best serves the purpose.

- **EVALUATE:** *Assess the credibility, currency, reliability, validity, and appropriateness of the information retrieved.*

Before the training manager actually uses the information, she must ensure that it is credible, current, reliable, and valid. For example, an information resource that provides market data from 2005 is not useful. Likewise, information published by a competing company may be biased. Credible resources must be used as a basis for making sound business decisions. The information-literate individual is able to assess the source of information for relevance appropriate to the needs of the current situation as well as evaluate sources for accuracy and conflicts of interest with present needs.

- **ORGANIZE:** *Compile the information so it can be used to meet the information need, solve the problem, or answer the question.*

  Once the training manager has gathered all of the needed information, she must organize it so it can be used to answer her specific questions. For example, she might want to show trends in population, the influx of new companies that require her training, and specific data showing that her training has little competition. Organizing the information according to each question will allow her to prepare her presentation more effectively.
- **COMMUNICATE:** *Communicate the information legally and ethically using a variety of channels directed at a range of audiences.*

  Finally, the training manager must communicate the information to the president and other decision makers in the company. She has been asked to make a formal presentation to a board of directors and will use charts, graphs, PowerPoint presentations, and other visual representations of the data. She also has been asked to write a formal proposal and will have to provide accurate information about her information sources. The training manager's ability to present the information clearly, using professional language, will be vital to her success. She must cite her sources accurately and present her references in a way that gives appropriate credit to her information sources.

Information literacy assumes several professional skills that are important to every successful student and professional. These skills, sometimes referred to as transferable skills, are abilities that are vital to career success, regardless of industry or job title. Critical thinking, creative thinking, problem solving, higher-order thinking, effective communication, and organization are transferable skills that provide a foundation for information literacy.

CRITICAL THINKING

By definition, critical thinking employs skills that contribute to information literacy. Critical thinking and information literacy both require distinguishing between assumption and fact, suspending personal opinion and bias in favor of objectivity, and considering issues from multiple perspectives and in adequate depth. The wealth of information available today from a wide variety of sources requires sharp analytical skills to determine both appropriateness and credibility. To achieve these objectives, one must think actively and systematically about information using a variety of strategies. Figure 1-1 illustrates only a few of the important critical thinking strategies. Critical thinking is more than just thinking, which sometimes can be biased, uninformed, distorted, superficial, or incomplete. Critical thinking is necessary for effective use of information.

The following processes involve critical thinking:

- **INFER:** *To draw conclusions from evidence or facts.*

  In the training company expansion case, the training manager responsible for the expansion inferred, from the

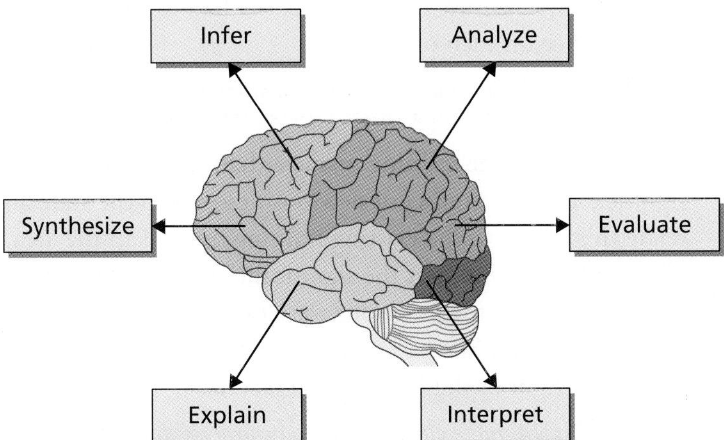

Figure 1-1 Critical Thinking Strategies. Critical thinking strategies can be categorized into six major areas.

lack of any significant training companies in the business directories she viewed, that her training company would have a good chance of being successful in the new state.

- **ANALYZE:** *To break down complex concepts into parts and then study how the parts are related to each other in making up the whole.*

  In the training company case, the training manager had to analyze the various data she found. For example, from all of the companies doing business in the new area, she had to identify those that might utilize her training. Her analysis involved multiple factors, including assessing the needs of companies and their ability to fund the training. She had to consider the perspectives of the decision makers in the companies, as well as the perspective of her own organization. She also had to find out how many other companies provide the same type of training. These are examples of the data analysis needed to make a good decision.

- **EVALUATE:** *To examine critically, given a specific set of criteria.*

  After broadly analyzing the training situation, the training manager had to critically examine the specific data, such as population statistics, marketing data, financial information, and the human resource requirements for the new training. In addition, to ensure effectiveness, she had to evaluate her performance on each of the steps.

- **INTERPRET:** *To comprehend the meaning or significance of something.*

  In the case, the training manager had to interpret the significance of the influx of new businesses into the state and relate this influx to the existing training options in the area. She also had to interpret the significance of the online training options and how these options were meeting the actual needs of the businesses. She had to consider the meaning of her analysis in light of these additional factors.

- **EXPLAIN:** *To make clear the thought process, facts, or concepts.*

  The training manager had to clearly explain and illustrate her recommendation to expand the company's training to the new state. She had to show how she arrived at the decision by presenting accurate, thorough, and effectively organized data.

- **SYNTHESIZE:** *To combine separate thoughts to form a concept.*
  Finally, to make a sound recommendation, the training manager had to take all of the information, including the recommendations of her subordinates, the state agency representatives she talked with, and potential customers, and combine this information with the empirical data (facts and figures) that she obtained in her research, to draw a logical and workable conclusion.

CREATIVE THINKING

Creative thinking is the process of actively exploring possibilities, generating alternatives, keeping an open mind toward change, and combining ideas to create something new or to view old concepts in new ways. The common phrase "think outside the box" refers to thinking creatively. Effective creative thinking is innovative, yet takes into consideration facts and realistic constraints. Creative thinkers use their imagination, are highly expressive, and are not restricted by existing ideas or barriers. They seek and embrace support from others to gain different perspectives.

For example, a construction foreman faced with increasing safety at the jobsite might hand out safety pamphlets and ask each laborer to read the information. A more creative solution, though, might be to create performance competition among three different teams by giving a safety quiz that identifies safety issues on the jobsite, and by rewarding the team that accrues the most points over the life of the project. Or the foreman might seek input from others to find out what safety programs have been effective in the past.

Effective information workers combine critical thinking and creative thinking in their approach to an information need or a problem-solving situation.

PROBLEM SOLVING

Problem solving entails a systematic process to find a solution to a question or an issue. Being information-literate requires knowing

1

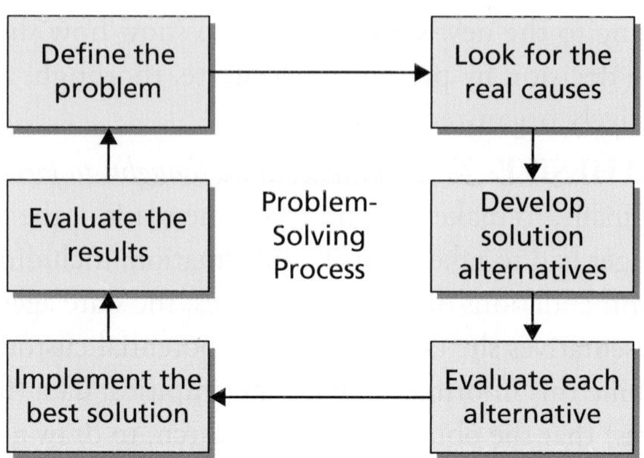

Figure 1-2 The Problem-Solving Process. Effective problem solving involves six major steps.

how to analyze and apply information to solve problems successfully. Steps in the problem-solving process consist of: (1) defining the problem, (2) looking for possible causes of the problem, (3) developing possible solutions to the problem, (4) evaluating each possible solution to determine the best one, (5) implementing the best solution, and (6) evaluating the results. Figure 1-2 illustrates a simplified version of this process.

- **DEFINE THE PROBLEM.** *A problem must be well understood before it can be solved. To define a problem, the training manager uses information to answer the questions: Who? What? Where? When? Why? How? How much?*

  As an example, consider an office network situation in which the process of backing up the information on the office network is inefficient and is taking too long. Most important, the system is ineffective, partially because of the office manager's lack of knowledge regarding traditional data backup equipment and the availability of cloud-based tools and resources. In this situation, the problem first must be defined by thoroughly reviewing the facts and assessing the processes used by the office manager who is responsible for the biweekly backups. Many of the files are crucial and contain information that, if lost, would cost the company money and time.

  In the current backup system, the office manager saves the latest files to a flash drive and takes the flash drive home to store the backups offsite for safekeeping. The problem is that this process is too time-consuming, the flash drive is not as reliable as other data-storage options over time, and the offsite storage is not secure.

- **LOOK FOR THE REAL CAUSES.** *Problem solvers have to ensure that they know the exact cause(s) of the problem and understand these causes thoroughly. With only a superficial study of the situation, the real causes of a problem may be hidden, so careful analysis and consideration of multiple perspectives may be necessary.*

  In the data-storage case, a closer look at this situation reveals that the office manager lacks knowledge about data backup and storage, and that using a flash drive is the only method he knows. At least part of the real cause of the problem is lack of skill on the part of the person responsible for the network and data.

- **DEVELOP SOLUTION ALTERNATIVES.** *Because getting input from appropriate people contributes to developing possible solutions, the problem solver has to engage others in brainstorming as part of the creative thinking process to generate as many alternatives as possible.*

  Among several potential options for solving the data backup and storage dilemma are: (1) the office manager could continue to use the flash drive as the backup and data-storage method; (2) the company could purchase a tape backup for data storage; (3) the company could purchase an external hard drive for backup and then store the hard drive offsite; and (4) the company could use a cloud backup and storage system offered by a third party. An issue related to both the problem and the solution is the need to provide the office manager with training on data backup and storage.

- **EVALUATE EACH ALTERNATIVE.** *The problem solver has to consider each alternative to determine which solution or combination of solutions works best. Getting an outside opinion from a neutral party contributes another perspective and additional data to the evaluation.*

  In the data backup and storage case, each alternative should be evaluated, using a set of predetermined criteria. Because the criteria and the questions asked vary with each situation, knowing the kind of information needed is necessary to define the relevant questions. In this case, the following questions are important: (1) How much does each system cost? (2) How reliable is each system, and how long does each system last? (3) How difficult is each system to implement and maintain? (4) How long does the actual backup process take? (5) How secure is each system? (6) What is the process for data recovery?

- **IMPLEMENT THE BEST SOLUTION.** *After selecting the best solution, the problem solver has to implement it carefully.*

  In the data backup and storage case, the company has chosen the solution of contracting with a third party for cloud backup and storage. Research revealed a relatively low cost, a high level of security and reliability, ease of implementation, and quick recovery of data, if needed. The company signed on with a reliable cloud backup and storage company and implemented the process within a few days. Also, the office manager received free training from that company on how to use the new system. He also learned how to increase the security and organization of the company's data and file system.

- **EVALUATE THE RESULTS.** *Finally, the problem solver has to assess whether the solution worked. Is the problem solved? If not, further evaluation is needed to determine what worked, what did not, and what changes are appropriate. He or she has to assess whether the information was adequate, whether it was used effectively, and whether the way the information was communicated influenced the outcome in any way. After any changes have been implemented, the cycle is repeated.*

  In the data backup and storage case, the company compared the results to the old system, assessed the overall security, and reviewed the existing data-management system. It was determined that, although the service did incur a monthly expense, the extra cost was offset by increased security and the office manager's increased efficiency. The company also decided to revisit the problem in one month to ensure that the data was being backed up as planned, and was stored appropriately.

HIGHER-ORDER THINKING

Higher-order thinking contributes to both critical and creative thinking processes. Bloom (1956) conceptualizes thinking as a pyramid having six levels, beginning with the lowest level (Knowledge) and

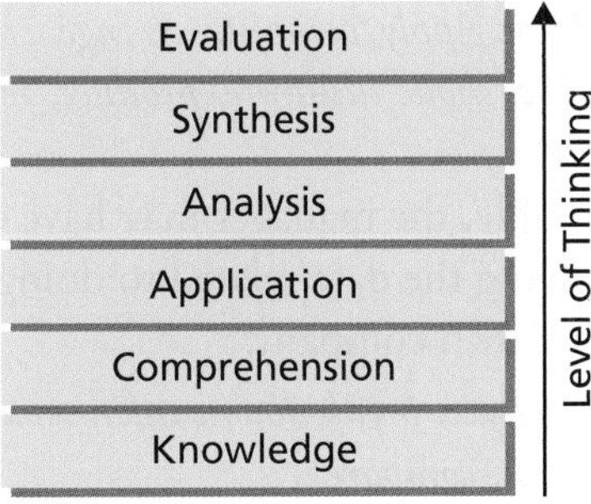

Figure 1-3 Bloom's Taxonomy. The six levels in Bloom's higher-order thinking taxonomy begin with broad, basic thinking (knowledge) and end with more advanced, complex thinking (evaluation).

increasing to the highest level (Evaluation). Each level describes a different way to think about information. The lowest level is superficial, considering straightforward facts. An example of this level is being able to name the states and their capitals. The highest level reflects deep, complex thinking, in which information is judged critically to reach a decision. The training company manager's process is an example of using the higher levels of Bloom's taxonomy.

The diagram in Figure 1-3 illustrates Bloom's taxonomy with its six levels of thinking about information. Information-literate individuals will use all levels of thinking at various times, depending on the information needed and the goal they are trying to achieve. Academic and professional activities tend to require the higher levels of thinking more often.

The following action verbs represent strategies for thinking effectively at each level of Bloom's taxonomy:

- **KNOWLEDGE:** *Define, identify, describe, recognize, label, list, match, name, reproduce, outline, recall.*

  In the training manager case introduced earlier in this chapter, knowledge is exemplified by the information regarding businesses, state laws and regulations, and other factual information relevant to her goal.

- **COMPREHENSION:** *Explain, generalize, extend, comprehend, give examples, summarize, translate, paraphrase, rewrite, predict.*

  An example of the comprehension level from this case is the manager pulling her factual data into a general statement to condense and summarize the information.

1

- **APPLICATION:** *Apply, compute, change, construct, develop, manipulate, solve, show, illustrate, produce, relate, use, operate, discover, modify.*

  In the example, the manager may have constructed scenarios, applying the data related to doing business in the new state to her own company.
- **ANALYSIS:** *Analyze, break down, infer, separate, diagram, differentiate, contrast, compare.*

  Following the application of the data to her own situation, the manager assessed her findings and compared and contrasted doing business in the new state with that in her current location.
- **SYNTHESIS:** *Categorize, generate, design, devise, compile, rearrange, reorganize, revise, reconstruct, combine, write, tell.*

  After completing her analysis, the manager compiled her conclusions and generated suggestions for following through on the project.
- **EVALUATION:** *Conclude, defend, critique, discriminate, judge, interpret, justify, support.*

  To conclude the process, the training manager critiqued her conclusions to ensure that they are logical and that her conclusions are sound.

Note that the level of thinking complexity increases when moving from basic knowledge to evaluation.

EFFECTIVE COMMUNICATION

Successful students and professionals must be able to communicate information effectively to many different types of audiences and in a variety of situations. To be able to communicate effectively, the sender of a message should understand the basic communication process shown in Figure 1-4.

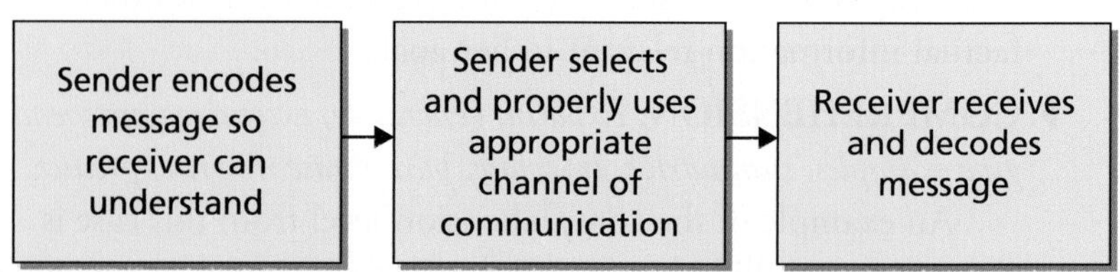

Figure 1-4 The Communication Process. The communication process involves a sender who encodes a message and then selects and utilizes an appropriate channel so a receiver can receive and decode the message.

The context in which communication occurs influences the way information and messages are used, expressed, and received. For example, your communication style in a group of friends is likely to differ from your communication style with a group of professors. One reason for this is that your friends and your professors belong to different audiences. You can communicate more effectively when you consider the audience you're speaking with.

Communicating to Various Audiences

The following brief scenario illustrates considering your audience and the basic communication process: Dr. Stewart has just received the results from a series of blood tests for her patient, John, who is suffering from extreme fatigue. Dr. Stewart has to tell John that he has hypoglycemia, a severely lowered blood glucose (blood sugar) level. First, Dr. Stewart must consider her audience. She is communicating with a member of the patient community (versus the medical community), so she must encode the message into a form that the receiver (John) can understand. Because John is not at all familiar with medical jargon, Dr. Stewart must use simple, layperson terms so John can clearly understand the details of his condition.

Next, Dr. Stewart must select and properly use a medium or channel to send this message. With confidential medical information, Dr. Stewart considers the most effective means to answer John's questions, in keeping with the Health Information Portability and Accountability Act (HIPAA), which provides legal and ethical guidelines on the dissemination of a patient's health information. Based on these considerations, Dr. Stewart decides to meet with John in person to answer his questions and maintain confidentiality. Dr. Stewart also decides to use an anatomical illustration of the digestive system and blood pathway as a visual aid to help John understand the importance of eating meals regularly. Finally, John must actually receive this information and decode it accurately so he will understand his medical condition.

Dr. Stewart has selected illustrations and explanations that are understandable to a member of the patient community. Consider how this might be different if Dr. Stewart were providing this information to a member of the medical community.

1

Self-Assessment Questions

- How do you think you might be asked to communicate new information in your workplace? List as many different ways or formats as you can. Be specific.
- Imagine yourself in the role of manager or owner of a company, organization, or facility similar to the kind in which you want to work during your career. Relative to information literacy, what information skills would you want your new employees to have? Why? As the owner or manager, how would you be at a disadvantage if your employees were information-illiterate? (Think about this question as you compare your facility to a competing facility with highly skilled employees in information areas.)

If any part of the communication process is missing or misunderstood, the message will not be communicated as intended. Accordingly, an effective communicator must develop specific skills related to each step in the communication process and be able to select the most effective approach based on the situation.

To encode and send a message successfully, the communicator must develop the abilities to:

- write well,
- organize information logically and coherently,
- speak in public,
- interact effectively with others,
- use visual elements in communicating an idea,
- use a variety of technologies (telephone, computer, email, cameras, audio and video recorders, etc.) to send the message.

A careful study of this process reveals that the sender is responsible for ensuring that the message is received as intended. The receiver also plays a role in the communication process by asking clarifying questions and actively participating in the conversation.

ORGANIZATION

A person who is organized has a systematic way to group information, takes notes on research so the main points can be identified, categorizes material so the information is easily found, and logs steps and resources for later reference. An information-literate individual must understand how to use a variety of organizational strategies to gather information and communicate it effectively. Specific skills include understanding and logically using electronic and print file management systems, practicing time-management techniques, breaking down complex tasks into manageable objectives, and appropriately using a variety of graphic organizers such as Venn diagrams, flowcharts, tables, Gantt charts, organizational charts, concept maps, and so forth. Each of these tools will be described later in the text.

Information literacy is an umbrella term that encompasses several types of literacy. An information-literate individual recognizes that all types of literacy are important and strives to become proficient in the skill sets required for each. These skill sets often overlap and support each other, and all rely on the transferable skills described earlier. The following types of literacy and their associated skills are important components of information literacy.

COMPUTER LITERACY

Computer literacy involves a basic understanding of how a computer works and how it can be applied to complete a task. A computer-literate individual understands the various terms associated with computer hardware, as well as common computer software applications. Figure 1-5 illustrates the various competency areas that make up computer literacy.

Purchasing a computer requires a student or professional to make many decisions regarding their current, as well as future, usage. Considerations include:

- The type and speed of the computer's processor.
- The amount of memory included.
- The type of operating system being installed (e.g., Windows, Mac, or Linux).

Mobility is also an important consideration. People who prefer to work in a consistent location often purchase a desktop computer,

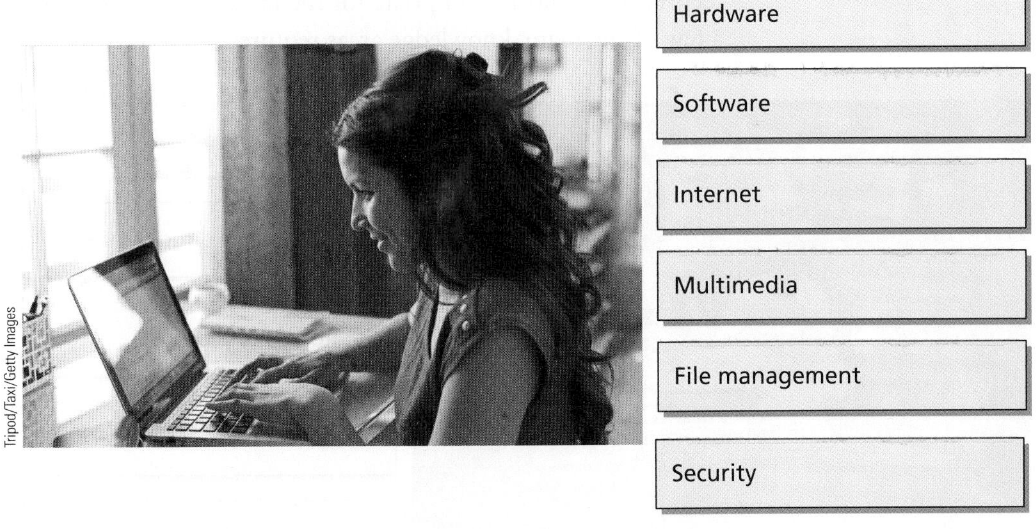

Figure 1-5 Computer Literacy Competencies. Computer literacy involves knowledge and skills in six major areas related to computers.

1

Self-Assessment Questions

- What is your preferred method for purchasing a computer? Do you do it online or would you rather buy a computer from a retail store?
- Are there specific apps that you consider to be absolutely necessary to be successful in college or the workplace?

whereas students and professionals who are on the go usually acquire a laptop, tablet, or both.

In addition to computers, students are increasingly using smartphones to complete research, access multimedia, and participate on social media sites. Relevant purchasing considerations include:

- The type of phone to purchase, such as an iPhone or Android.
- The voice and data plan.
- Whether or not to use a provider that requires a contract.

In addition to the decisions listed above, total cost of ownership is an important consideration when purchasing any type of technology.

LIBRARY LITERACY

Library literacy encompasses an understanding of the different kinds of information resources housed in a library—books, encyclopedias, catalogs, periodicals, audio and video resources, and so forth. Library literacy also includes knowing how to locate the resources in the library, understanding how to find and access information within each resource, being knowledgeable about correct referencing processes, and being able to get help from a librarian when necessary. Today, libraries use both print and sophisticated electronic resources and search tools. An important aspect of library literacy is to know which technology is most appropriate for the task. Figure 1-6 illustrates only a few of the many knowledge areas required for library literacy.

Bananastock Ltd./Jupiter Images

Books and periodicals

Databases and directories

Catalogs and indexes

Media resources

Reference materials

Figure 1-6 Knowledge Areas of Library Literacy. Library literacy involves knowledge and skills in five major areas.

1

MEDIA LITERACY

One definition of media literacy is provided by the Center for Media Literacy (n.d.):

> "Media Literacy is a 21st-century approach to education. It provides a framework to access, analyze, evaluate, create, and participate using messages in a variety of forms—from print to video to the Internet. Media literacy builds an understanding of the role of the media in society as well as essential skills of inquiry and self-expression necessary for citizens of a democracy."

The information-literate individual must understand the many options available and know how to translate the information into the best choice. Media-literate individuals also understand the advantages, disadvantages, challenges, and purposes of each type of media.

VISUAL LITERACY

A component of media literacy is visual literacy: the ability to use visual media effectively to learn and communicate (International Visual Learning Association, 2012). We live in an increasingly visual culture, and the information-literate person recognizes that understanding how to view, interpret, and produce visual media is paramount. Though information-literate individuals do not have to be graphic designers or accomplished artists, in many cases visual elements are the best choice for conveying a message. Information-literate individuals must understand how to find, create, format, alter, and embed visual elements into the message, using basic computer software and other tools.

SELF-ASSESSMENT QUESTIONS

- Review the following quote: "In this knowledge-oriented workplace, information literacy is the key to power." What does this mean to you in your own career path? Write down some specific examples of how this might be true for you.
- Reflect on your area of study and the job-related tasks in your current or future career. What sources and information will you have to be able to locate, access, retrieve, and use? List as many different areas and types of information as you can. Expand this list as you think of additional types of information and sources.

TECHNOLOGY LITERACY

Finally, the information-literate individual must be able to use a variety of technologies to find and access information, as well as to effectively organize, use, and communicate information. These skills make up technology literacy. Included in technology skills are the ability to use basic computer software programs (e.g., word processing, spreadsheets, presentation tools, databases), the Internet, social media, and supporting tools such as search engines, file-management systems, blogs, Really Simple Syndication (RSS) feeds, and so forth.

1

Critical Thinking Questions

- If a workplace professional were said to be computer-literate, how would you describe his or her skills specifically?
- Assuming that you are not the librarian but are said to be a great researcher and literate in using the library, what kind of skills would you have?
- To be media-literate, what specific workplace or school situations might you participate in? What specific skills would you have?
- Think about the careers that intrigue you and where you might see yourself working. How might you have to be visually literate? How would this help you communicate or achieve some other workplace or school goal?
- What skills do you think are essential for someone who is visually literate? Do these skills differ in different career areas?

And, because technology changes quickly, information-literate individuals must update their technology skills continuously to stay current and be able to use their existing skills in new ways.

Information literacy is not just for the technical student or the business and technology professional. Information skills are required in every career, and continued growth of this trend can be expected. For example, health professions (which at one time were considered "nontechnical") are now using technology for managing patient records, charting patient progress, and operating equipment. In fact, a key provision of the American Recovery and Reinvestment Act of 2009 made it a requirement that healthcare providers begin using electronic medical records (EMR) by January of 2014.

All professionals rely on some type of information to complete their job tasks successfully. To be successful in a career, the college graduate no longer can rely solely on the information learned in school. As information is changing constantly, today's professionals must acquire new knowledge and skills continuously. For example, an allied health professional will have to keep up with new procedures, medication, diseases, and treatments. A construction professional must keep up with new materials, codes, and techniques. A business professional must be able to gather data on markets, the competition, and new avenues for products and services. Technology has resulted in information being easily updated. The successful professional knows how to use technology to access information that is constantly being added to the body of knowledge in every field. Individuals who lack information literacy skills may rely on outdated information and data, and as a result, be hindered significantly in job success and advancement.

CASE IN POINT: SEEK AND YE SHALL FIND

Read the following scenario. Then, in groups or as a class, discuss the questions at the end.

Derrick Washington just graduated from college with an associate degree in nursing and was hired at a long-term nursing facility as a caregiver. This facility has the philosophy that true patient care stems from a genuine concern for each individual patient and in-depth knowledge about the individual diseases and disorders challenging each patient. In light of this philosophy, the administration asks all staff members, regardless of position, to attend weekly in-service training sessions to learn more about the care of patients. The staff members take turns presenting information about selected diseases, disorders, and other healthcare issues, including healthcare ethics, legal issues, economic issues, related community issues, aging issues, communication topics, and diversity topics.

Each staff member is assigned a topic and is asked to fully research the subject, select the most relevant information for the staff as a whole, develop a one- to two-page information sheet with a "Resources for Additional Learning" section, and create a "Tips for Patient Education" page for distribution to each staff member. In addition, staff members are required to deliver a 20-minute presentation on their topic to the entire group of care providers. All staff members are expected to participate, provide current and accurate information, and use excellent professional communication skills.

The facility administration considers these in-service training sessions as essential to the facility's continued excellence and as a contributing factor in salary increases and promotions. Accordingly, all staff members are assessed quarterly on the effectiveness of the in-services they have given during the quarter. All staff members are expected to achieve 80 percent or better on these assessments.

Through self-reflection and honest evaluation, Derrick has found that he does not have the information skills required to excel in this workplace expectation. He realizes that he does not know how to determine what kind of information he will need for the in-services, how to find current information efficiently, or how to assess the credibility of information. In addition, he does not feel confident in his ability to organize the information effectively into a brief written summary or to make a professional presentation, even though he took related courses for these skills in school. He is significantly stressed about this employment requirement.

- If assigned a professional task, how would you use the Internet and library services to find the necessary information in an efficient manner?
- How would you know that the information you find is credible?
- What methods would you use to pull significant points from a large body of information and organize them into a presentation that is engaging and teaches your colleagues?
- What steps should Derrick take to improve upon his information skills?
- How could the administration help in increasing Derrick's information skills to the level that is necessary in their workplace?

STEPS IN EFFECTIVE RESEARCH

Successfully using information to meet a need can be defined in the series of steps illustrated in Figure 1-7. The remainder of this text discusses factors contributing to each step in detail and explores the related information skills.

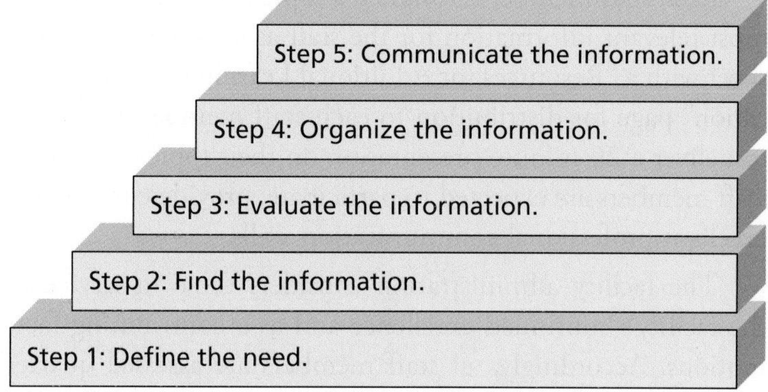

Figure 1-7 Steps in Effective Research. There are five steps to effective research.

STEP 1: DEFINE THE NEED AND THE AUDIENCE

Before even beginning to seek the proper information, individuals must establish and articulate the need for that information. This requires consulting with appropriate individuals to communicate and define the need. A need can be a problem that must be solved, a question that must be answered, or a task that must be performed. For example, an instructor may assign to students the task of writing an essay on a controversial issue. In this case, information is needed to describe each side of the issue in depth. The student also must be able to communicate the information in the required format. In the workplace, a departmental team may be asked to solve a production problem. In this case, the information need is to find information about potential technology solutions and then to evaluate which solution is the best option in light of the company's financial and time constraints. Finally, the team must communicate this solution to decision makers.

questions to ask to define the need and the audience

- What kind of information do I need? (facts, figures, statistics, opinions, sides of an issue, historical or background, profile, interview, primary, secondary, etc.)
- How much information do I need? (limited scope, in-depth coverage, summary or overview, etc.)
- What parameters should I follow? (time period, geographical location, age or gender, point of view, etc.)
- Who will be receiving this information? (practitioners, professionals, laypeople, scientists, team members, colleagues, clients, patients, etc.)

CRITICAL THINKING QUESTIONS

- An obsolete employee is one who no longer has the skills required to do the job. What specifically might an obsolete employee in your career field look like in 10 years?
- How do ambitious employees prevent themselves from becoming obsolete? Be specific, and relate your ideas specifically to your field of study.

STEP 2: FIND THE INFORMATION

Step 2 involves creating a research strategy customized to the task at hand. A research strategy is a kind of map that is used to avoid wasting time and wandering aimlessly through the massive amounts of information available in libraries, on the Internet, and elsewhere. A research strategy includes deciding what resources to use, whether the resources are available and cost-effective, if using specific resources provides significant benefit, how the resources can be accessed, and the timeline required to accomplish the research. To develop this map, the information gatherer must understand how information is produced, organized, and communicated, in both formal and informal situations.

With a plan in hand, the information gatherer then must call upon a variety of information skills to conduct the research. This step assumes an understanding of how to locate information using search tools and information-retrieval systems, how to apply appropriate investigative methods to obtain the best information, how to find the information within a given resource, how to take useful notes, and how to extract information and save it in an organized manner.

questions to ask to find useful information

- What information sources should I use? (encyclopedias, professional journals, people, directories, databases, popular magazines, maps, videos, etc.)
- Where do I find these resources? (library, Internet, individuals, companies, government resources, librarian, etc.)
- How do I search for the information within each resource? (index, electronic search engine, etc.)
- How should I retrieve the information once I find it? (download, photocopy, interlibrary loan, print, etc.)
- How should I manage the information that I retrieve? (electronic files, print file folders, etc.)

STEP 3: EVALUATE THE INFORMATION

Evaluating the research results requires the information gatherer to apply a set of criteria to determine if the information is reliable, valid, accurate, current, and free from bias. In this part of the evaluation, the credibility of the actual information sources is assessed. Information also must be evaluated to determine if it meets the research need. This type of evaluation requires filtering, from all of the collected data, information that is important to the original question or problem.

In the next chapters, we will define more extensively what is involved in answering each of these questions.

questions to ask to evaluate information effectively

- Is the information current?
- Is the information credible?
- Is the information accurate?
- Is the information relevant to the need?
- Is the information useful?
- Is the information free from bias?

STEP 4: ORGANIZE THE INFORMATION

An information-literate individual uses systematic strategies to organize information so it can be communicated in the most effective way. Organization starts with managing the information retrieved in the research process. For many research projects, a large amount of information is available, some of which may not be useful or directly related to the need. Sometimes it is difficult to know if all of the information is important until the information gathering is complete. Keeping information organized as it is collected simplifies the evaluation process. Information also must be organized to achieve the communication goal. Information can be organized and presented according to several criteria, which will be discussed in-depth in the Organizing Information chapter.

questions to ask to organize information effectively

- How do I organize the information so I can find main ideas, key issues, different viewpoints, etc.?
- How can I think about the information in new ways?
- How should I manage a large amount of information?
- How do I organize the information so it is presented logically and appropriately? (chronologically, priority of elements, problem/solution, deductive order, inductive order, etc.)

STEP 5: COMMUNICATE THE INFORMATION

The information-literate individual must communicate the information to others effectively so it can be used to solve the problem, answer the question, or meet the original need. Effective communication considers many factors and can be transmitted through a variety of channels: written documents, verbal presentations, visual presentations, and a variety of electronic formats. The communication also must be legal and ethical according to copyright laws, intellectual property standards, and the accurate citation of information sources.

Finally, the entire research process and results should be evaluated to determine if the information has met the need sufficiently, solved the problem, or answered the original questions. If not, the process should be evaluated and changes made if appropriate.

questions to ask to communicate information effectively

- Who is my audience? Am I communicating on a casual topic or for business? Is the setting formal or relaxed? The type of audience and the setting will determine how to deliver the information.
- What channel should be used to communicate the research results? (written, verbal, visual, electronic, etc.)
- For the selected channel, what specific format best meets the communication need? (proposal, narrative, research report, slide presentation, image, diagram, etc.)
- How do I properly reference the resources I use and give appropriate credit to the original authors of the information?

SELF-ASSESSMENT QUESTIONS

- Which steps in the research process do you think you currently do well?
- In which steps do you think you need to develop more knowledge and skill?
- What do you think are the most difficult steps for you to complete? Why?
- What do you think are the easiest steps for you to complete? Why?

success steps for effective research

- Define the need and the audience.
- Find the information.
- Evaluate the information.
- Organize the information.
- Communicate the information.

CHAPTER SUMMARY

This chapter introduced you to the concept of information literacy. You now are familiar with what you need to do to be an information-literate individual and why being information-literate is important to your success. Conversely, you are aware of the challenges that can face an individual who is not.

POINTS TO KEEP IN MIND

- Information literacy is the ability to locate, access, retrieve, evaluate, use, and communicate information effectively.
- The information-literate individual has the knowledge to locate, access, retrieve, evaluate, use, and effectively communicate information.
- Information literacy is essential to success in school and in the workplace.

apply it

- Define *information literacy*.
- Name the specific skills required for an individual to be an information-literate student or professional.
- Explain the importance of knowing how to locate, access, retrieve, evaluate, use, and effectively communicate information in school and in the workplace.
- Outline the challenges facing an individual who does not possess information skills in school and in the workplace.

Activity #1: Self-Analysis: Research Process

GOAL: To reflect critically on your current process for finding and using information and to generate a list of areas for improvement.

Think carefully and write down your answers to each of the following questions:

1. When you are given a research task, what typically is your first step? Then what do you do? Sketch your personal and realistic research process from beginning to end.
2. What resources do you typically use to find information? List each resource you have used in recent years (e.g., Internet, encyclopedia, dictionary, journal, newspaper, directory).
3. What resources do you commonly use in a library?
4. What search tools are you proficient at using (printed and/or electronic)?
5. How specifically do you copy down and organize the information you find?
6. How do you organize your electronic files on your computer?
7. On a scale from 1 to 5 where 1 = need significant improvement and 5 = expert, rate yourself in each of the following areas. Be honest.

Rating Table

Area	Rating 1–5
Critical thinking	
Creative thinking	

continued

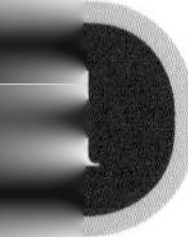

continued

Area	Rating 1–5
Problem solving	
Higher-order thinking	
Effective communication	
Organization	
Computer literacy	
Library literacy	
Media literacy	
Visual literacy	
Technology literacy	
Effective research	

Activity #2: Predicting the Future of Information

GOAL: To emphasize the importance of information literacy for the future.

STEP 1: Brainstorm answers to the following questions. Use your imagination. Think critically and creatively. Remember that in brainstorming, the goal is to generate as many ideas as possible but not to judge or evaluate these ideas.

- What will libraries look like in 10 years? In 20 years?
- How will people communicate with each other in 10 years? In 20 years?
- What will computers look like in 10 years? What will they be able to do that they cannot do now? In 20 years?

STEP 2: Organize your list into descriptive categories, and be prepared to compare your list with those of others.

Activity #3: Web Research

GOAL: To develop a full understanding of the importance of information literacy in career success.

STEP 1: Go to the American Library Association's website: www.ala.org

STEP 2: Once there, use the site's search tool to find the Information Literacy resources. Read the information provided.

STEP 3: Go to Google and complete a search for "information literacy." Explore at least two additional websites related to information literacy. What are others doing in the area of information literacy, and how do they describe the various skill sets?

STEP 4: List at least 20 specific skills that you need to personally develop related to finding, accessing, retrieving, evaluating, using, and communicating information. Be prepared to share your list with your classmates.

STEP 5: Place the List of 20 Information Skills You Need to Develop in your Learning Portfolio.

SUGGESTED ITEMS FOR LEARNING PORTFOLIO

Refer to the "How to Use This Book" section at the beginning of this textbook for more information on learning portfolios.

- List of 20 Information Skills You Know You Need to Develop.

REFERENCES

American Library Association (ALA). (2000). *Information Literacy Competency Standards for Higher Education.* Retrieved June 10, 2013, from http://www.ala.org/ala/mgrps/divs/acrl/standards/standards.pdf

American Library Association Digital Literacy Task Force. (2013). *Digital Literacy, Libraries, and Public Policy.* Retrieved June 5, 2013, from http://www.districtdispatch.org/wp-content/uploads/2013/01/2012_OITP_digilitreport_1_22_13.pdf

Bloom, B. S. (1956). *Taxonomy of Educational Objectives, Handbook I: The Cognitive Domain.* New York: David McKay.

Center for Media Literacy. (n.d.). *What is Media Literacy? A Definition... and More.* Retrieved June 10, 2013, from http://www.medialit.org/reading-room/what-media-literacy-definitionand-more

Infogineering.net. (n.d.). *The Eight Must-Have Skills for Information Workers.* Retrieved June 7, 2013, from http://www.infogineering.net/information-worker-skills.htm

International Visual Learning Association. (2012). *What is "visual literacy?"* Retrieved June 10, 2013, from http://ivla.org/new/what-is-visual-literacy-2/

Jones, B. and Flannigan, S. (n.d.). *Connecting the Digital Dots: Literacy of the 21st Century.* Retrieved June 6, 2013, from http://www.nmc.org/pdf/Connecting%20the%20Digital%20Dots.pdf

Rasmus, D. (2012). *What is an Information Worker?* Retrieved February 7, 2016, from http://www.seriousinsights.net/what-is-an-information-worker/

Wesleyan University. (2016). *Information literacy.* Retrieved February 23, 2016, from http://www.wesleyan.edu/libr/infoforyou/infolitdefined.html

CHAPTER OUTLINE

Determining the Information You Need

LEARNING OBJECTIVES

By the end of this chapter, you will be able to:

- Explain the need for a main research question and relevant, focused research questions.
- Develop effective main research questions and focused research questions.
- Distinguish between primary and secondary sources.
- Explain various ways to present information.
- Explain various ways to access information.
- Identify and describe information sources.

2

BE IN THE KNOW

Primary Source Analysis Tool

As you will learn in this chapter, the use of primary and secondary sources will be critical to your research efforts as you go through school.

The Library of Congress (www.loc.gov) has devised a Primary Source Analysis Tool that can help you review primary source materials and to assess their value as they pertain to the research topic. This tool can be accessed at www.loc.gov/teachers/primary-source-analysis-tool/.

Once you have completed your analysis online, your results can be downloaded, printed, or emailed using the links at the bottom of the page.

As you start research on a topic, consider using this handy tool online. It may just be the jumpstart your project needs.

SOLVING INFORMATION PROBLEMS: DEFINING THE NEED AND THE AUDIENCE

One of the most daunting tasks that college students face during their academic careers is writing research papers. Even if writing comes easily to you, there is still the matter of deciding on a topic, identifying your audience, defining the need for your paper (in other words, what you want to accomplish by writing it), choosing your writing style, and identifying sources of information that are credible and reliable.

To be efficient, you first must clearly define the concepts relevant to your topic and the related information need. A need can be a problem that must be solved, a question that must be answered, or a task that must be performed. This need must be defined and communicated clearly. This is the first step to conducting effective research, as shown in Figure 2-1.

Self-Assessment Questions

Think of situations you have been in that require information on subjects you know nothing about.

- What process did you use to learn more about the subject?
- Did you have a plan?
- What steps did you follow to find the information you needed?

DEFINING A TOPIC

In school, your research topic most likely will be determined by its relevance to the assignment. Your instructor may assign a specific topic or give you a range of topics from which to choose. Examples of other criteria for selecting topics are current events, current needs in a

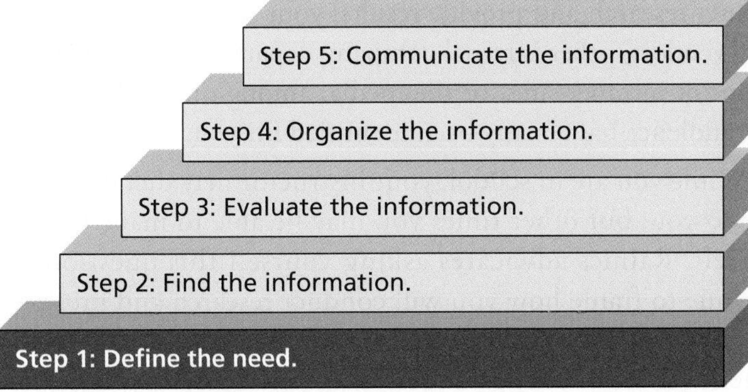

Figure 2-1 Research Process Step 1: Define the Need. The first step of any research project should be to clearly define what is needed.

field, organizational goals and priorities, market trends, and training needs. These topics are more relevant to the workplace and represent research that you might undertake later in your career. The criteria for selecting a topic will depend largely on your field, organizational needs, and audience.

IDENTIFYING YOUR WRITING STYLE

Now that you have successfully defined your research topic and the related informational need, it is important to establish the writing style that you will use for your paper.

Ann Raimes in her text *Keys for Writers* suggests the following writing styles be used for research papers based upon the need.

- If the main purpose of your research paper is to inform or explain an idea to the reader, then use *informative* (also known as *expository*) *writing*.
- If your paper's goal is to persuade readers to see your point of view or to spur them into action, use a *persuasive writing* style.
- If you are writing about an experiment or laboratory results, or are describing a detailed process, then a *technical* or *scientific writing* style should be employed (Raimes, 2013).

DEFINING THE AUDIENCE

At this stage of the writing process, you should define your audience. In the workplace, there are many audiences for whom you may conduct research and provide results: your supervisor, clients, third-party vendors, other internal company departments, company publications or intranet sites, or the media, among others. In these cases, your audience has already been identified for you.

While you are in school, your instructor may dictate your audience to you, but other times you may be able to make that choice yourself. Raimes advocates asking yourself this question as you continue to frame how you will conduct research and present your information: "how will reading my paper change or affect how my audience thinks, feels, or understands my topic?" (Raimes, 2013).

By defining your topic and your audience and identifying the writing style best suited to both, you will be well on your way to solving an information problem.

THE MAIN RESEARCH QUESTION

One of the best ways to further define your topic is to formulate a main research question as a starting point for the research. This question should include the key terms or concepts that are relevant to your topic. An effective research question will not be so broad that you have too much information to sort through, and will not be so narrow that you are confined in your research. It should direct your research appropriately for your topic and your audience. Time and effort spent on developing an effective research question will save time and effort later in the research process.

Review the following examples of effective and ineffective research questions.

Effective research questions:

1. What effect does divorce have on academic achievement in elementary school children?
2. How has global warming affected the size of the polar ice cap?
3. What are the differences between the various processors available for computers?

Ineffective research questions:

1. Who was Benjamin Franklin?
2. Should older people be allowed to drive?
3. Does the United States have a good foreign policy?

An effective research question poses a question that can be answered with verifiable facts. It is phrased in a way that avoids opinions. It is sufficiently specific to address the real need or purpose of the research. For example, effective research question #1 is specific. The answer to this question can be formed by searching electronic, library, and other information resources to find verifiable facts. If no information is available, a study can be conducted to compare the academic performance of children from divorced parents with the academic performance of children from two-parent families. If the study is conducted properly, using sound scientific investigative methods, the result should be useful information about how divorce affects academic performance in children.

By contrast, ineffective research question #1 (about Benjamin Franklin) is too broad to be useful in directing the research process. Benjamin Franklin's life has many facets. The best answer to this question depends on the purpose of the information. If you are collecting information on American statesmen, you would focus on the political life of Franklin. If you want information on inventors, you would describe Franklin by looking at his scientific endeavors. Perhaps your goal is to compile a general biography about influential Americans. Your perspective would be different, and you would seek different kinds of information from different information sources. Until the question is narrowed, you cannot search effectively for information or conduct research. You also would organize the information differently depending on which aspect of Benjamin Franklin's life is selected.

Now look at ineffective research question #2 (about older people driving). This question is also too vague to be effective and is phrased in a way that solicits opinion, not fact. For example, if you were to ask this question to a group of older people (or related information sources), you might get an entirely different answer than if you were to ask the question to a group of individuals who have had loved ones injured or killed by an older driver. The question also lacks a definition of "older," as well as criteria for assessment. The question is closed-ended, meaning that it is phrased in such a way that solicits a brief yes-or-no response.

Ineffective research question #3 (about foreign policy) is vague, broad, and subjective. What aspect of foreign policy is in question?

2

From whose perspective should the question be answered? Which political party? Which country? What is the purpose of the question? When additional questions such as these are necessary to understand the research question, the research question may be too general and broad. Answering the additional questions provides direction to your research project.

Keep in mind that opinion and judgment are different. Both are subjective in nature because they each require your ideas and thoughts, but judgment is supported by facts and verifiable data—opinion is not. In college and in the workplace, you may be asked for your judgment on a topic or issue. For example, at school you may have to write a position paper in which you are asked to state and support your stance on a topic. In the workplace, you may be asked to provide a recommendation for a course of action. To be considered a reliable researcher, you must use relevant facts to support your stance. Doing so distinguishes judgment from your opinion and contributes to your credibility and professional advancement.

Critical Thinking Questions

- What are the differences between the effective and ineffective questions?
- How would you make the three ineffective research questions effective?
- How do the three effective research questions help in planning the research process?

questions to ask to define a research question

- Is the research question specific enough?
- Does the question elicit fact or opinion?
- Can the research question be answered with verifiable facts?

FOCUSED RESEARCH QUESTIONS

Once you have formulated your main research question, the next step is to break it down into more detailed questions, called focused research questions. Focused research questions break down the main question by asking *who*, *what*, *where*, *when*, *why*, and *how*. These questions keep the research directed to the specifics of the topic and purpose of the question. They allow the researcher to develop a well-planned and efficient search strategy.

Review the following focused research questions, which have been developed for the following main research question.

Does exercise level positively or negatively impact food consumption in obese individuals?

Effective focused questions:

- What is the definition of an obese individual?
- What is the definition of exercise?
- How is exercise measured?
- Do obese individuals who increase their level of exercise increase or decrease their food intake measured in calories?
- What level of exercise shows a change in food intake?

These focused questions allow you to make a plan for researching the main question. They give you a start on identifying specific resources you can use to find the information. By answering the focused questions, you can begin to organize your thoughts, back up your ideas with information, and logically and reasonably answer the main research question.

Self-Assessment Questions

Think about a research project you have completed in the past.

- What is an effective research question?
- What are good focused questions you could have asked for this project?

questions to ask to define a focused research question

- Do my focused questions direct me to the specifics of the question?
- Do my focused research questions address the purpose of the question?
- Do my focused research questions organize my thoughts about the question and direct my research activity?

CASE IN POINT: LET ME ENTERTAIN YOU

As a recent college graduate, Rachael Burgess was eager to start her new job at an event management company as the meeting manager and administrative assistant. On her first day, Rachael's supervisor asked her to research on-site entertainment for a client who was going to be holding a sales meeting at a nearby resort in six months.

continued

2

Eager to impress her supervisor with a quick turnaround of information, and using her computer savvy, Rachael did an Internet search of entertainment options in the city where the resort was located, and presented the top three search results to her boss within 30 minutes of the request.

- Aside from using a search engine, what other sources of information could Rachael have used to locate the information her supervisor requested?
- What focused research questions could Rachael have asked about the client's request? How might asking focused research questions affect Rachael's search for information?
- How reliable and credible do you think information is that comes from being a top search item on the Internet?
- Do you think the quickest research results are always the best and most accurate?
- Could Rachael use social media sites to find more information about entertainment options?

PRIMARY AND SECONDARY SOURCES

Information sources can be categorized as primary or secondary. Primary sources are those that are closest to the actual event, time period, or individual in question. The information in these sources has not been edited, interpreted, condensed, or evaluated in a way that might change the original information. Primary sources also present original thinking and observations, such as the initial research used to write journal articles reporting on first-hand scientific studies, experiments, or observations.

Examples of primary sources:

- memoirs
- diaries
- autobiographies
- interviews with people
- public records

- transcripts of speeches
- letters, emails, memos, electronic mailing lists, blogs, discussion threads, newsgroups, and other correspondences
- discussions and electronic discussions on the Internet
- meetings and minutes taken at meetings
- newspaper articles reporting at the time of the event
- surveys
- government documents
- artifacts
- photographs and works of art
- observations
- patents
- works of literature, such as fiction and poems

Secondary sources are those that are removed from the primary source. Authors of secondary sources examine, interpret, or reflect on the primary source information to restate or reuse the information. These types of sources are more widely available than primary sources and are sometimes easier to use, but they should be evaluated critically to ensure that the author of a secondary source has not misinterpreted or altered the original information to support a specific opinion or viewpoint. Whenever possible, it is wise to locate the primary source in the references of the secondary source, and to give credit to both in your citations.

Examples of secondary sources:

- books and textbooks
- review articles from scholarly journals
- scientific reports (articles in scholarly journals that describe an original research study, experiment, or observation)
- technical reports
- conference papers and proceedings
- theses and dissertations
- handbooks
- databases
- catalogs and other indexing and abstracting tools used to locate information

- newspaper articles that analyze events
- dictionaries and encyclopedias
- magazine articles
- newspapers
- audio files, CD-ROMs, DVDs, Blu-Rays, and online media sources that have been edited

Use of inaccurate or misleading secondary information can compromise your research. Keep in mind that all information has the potential to influence some behavior. Therefore, you must ensure that you use information that is accurate, credible, and complete. The Evaluating Information chapter further addresses ways to determine the credibility of information.

Critical Thinking Questions

- Of the two types of information sources, primary and secondary, which do you think is more accessible? Why?
- What specific primary sources might be available for your field of study? List as many examples as you can.
- What specific secondary sources are available for your field of study? List as many examples as you can.
- What are potential issues with using any of these secondary sources for your field of study?

LIBRARY INFORMATION SOURCES

Once you have clearly defined the information need in terms of a main research question and appropriate focused questions, it is time to move to Step 2 in the information process, as shown in Figure 2-2. Finding the information incorporates two different skills:

1. Being aware of the various sources of information available.
2. Knowing how to locate and access the information in your sources.

Self-Assessment Question

- What types of primary source information would authors have at their disposal to research your life?

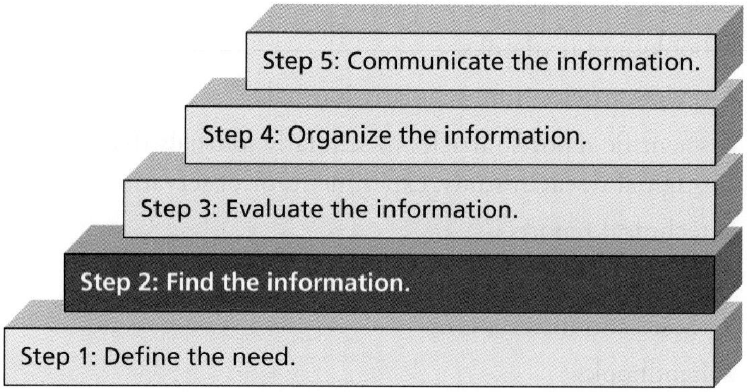

Step 5: Communicate the information.
Step 4: Organize the information.
Step 3: Evaluate the information.
Step 2: Find the information.
Step 1: Define the need.

Figure 2-2 Research Process Step 2: Find the Information. The second step of any research project should be to find the information efficiently.

Identifying the sources of information that are useful in academic and workplace research is a critical step in conducting an effective information search. Knowledge of information sources available in libraries and on the Internet is the foundation of library literacy, an important component of information literacy.

BOOKS

Books are common and convenient sources of information. Books can be fiction (content that is based on imagination and not necessarily on fact) or nonfiction (information that is factual). They are available on every subject of interest and many can be found in most libraries or downloaded as e-books.

Because of the significant time lapse between the time a book is written and its publication, certain types of information found in books may be outdated. For example, information in a book on human anatomy will be valid for years to come, as anatomy does not change quickly. Conversely, a book on computer software is likely to be outdated quickly because of the nature of the information and the rapidly changing technical world. When you select a book as a reference, you will have to use good judgment about the kind of information you are seeking. In the example of computer software, a better and more current choice would be technical documentation from the most recent version of the software you are researching.

Fiction

The primary purpose of a work of fiction is entertainment. Fiction gives the reader the opportunity to see problems and solutions through the actions of the character(s). The reader can live vicariously through the novel's characters and gain insight into "real-life" situations without repercussion. Figure 2-3 outlines the elements of fiction.

Historical fiction is based on an event or a sequence of events in history that actually occurred, but the author re-creates action and emotion through his or her imagination to tell the story of the event or of the characters.

2

Elements of a Fiction Novel	
Character(s)	Solution to the problem
Plot	Tone/mood
Theme	Symbolism
Setting	Imagery
Point of view	Figurative language
Basic problem	

Figure 2-3 Elements of a Fiction Novel. Numerous elements in a fiction work differentiate it from nonfiction.

Nonfiction

Nonfiction presents factual information. Nonfiction books are based on research and events that have occurred, and characters or objects that exist now or have existed in the past. Critical evaluation of the information given in a nonfiction resource is vital to the credibility of a research project. Elements that should be considered in light of the goal of your research include the author's background, purpose for writing the book, and attitude, as well as the audience for which the work is written. See Figure 2-4 for examples of elements of nonfiction. Evaluation of nonfiction information will be discussed in-depth in the Evaluating Information chapter.

Self-Assessment Question

- In your profession or field of study, do you use any books with information that remains relevant and does not become outdated?

Elements of Nonfiction	
Facts	Direct quotes
Characters (Real)	Illustrations
First person accounts	Timelines
Actual events	Maps
Actual places	Table of contents
Photographs	Bibliography
Archival material	Glossary
Charts	Index
Diagrams	

Figure 2-4 Elements of Nonfiction. The elements commonly seen in nonfiction are more factual than creative.

REFERENCE SOURCES

A library typically has a reference or information desk that is staffed by a reference librarian. You can use these services to get answers to questions or to receive assistance with your research needs. The professionally trained librarians will help you find the kind of information sources that best meet your needs by conducting a reference interview. In many libraries, you can also call, email, or use online chat to get help.

Use the reference desk to:

- get help finding a library resource.
- get the answer to a specific, factual question.
- get assistance in using the online public access catalog (OPAC) or other library computer resources.
- access the ready reference collection, which contains books that are commonly referenced.
- access rare or restricted items in the library.
- locate difficult-to-find information.
- put a library resource on hold when an item you need is temporarily unavailable (i.e., checked out by another patron); the librarian will notify you when the resource has been returned.
- access resources that instructors have set aside for a specific project or for a specific time period.
- discover items in the library that are not cataloged in the OPAC, such as old telephone books, college-course catalogs, and school yearbooks.
- sign up for use of library equipment, such as microfilm readers or computers.
- make a recommendation that the library purchase something for its collection.
- gain access to locked or reserved study or conference rooms.
- get recommendations on specific resources to meet a specific research need.
- get recommendations for useful websites or advice on searching the Internet.
- get a referral to a different library that has additional resources to meet your needs.
- request a resource from another library through the interlibrary loan system.

A reference source is material from which information can be drawn. Reference sources are authoritative and frequently subject-specific. These sources include reference books, records from library catalogs, general or subject-specific indexes, and bibliographic databases. Many reference materials are available in both print and electronic formats and are often accessible through a local library computer system or via the Internet. Reference sources may provide actual information, or they may be used to find additional information sources. Some of the more commonly available and useful reference sources are described next. Typically, reference books must be used in the library and cannot be checked out. In most cases, you can make copies of the information you need, provided that you observe copyright restrictions.

Encyclopedias

An encyclopedia is a collection of detailed articles on a wide range of subjects. Encyclopedias are typically used to find background information on a subject. They can be general (e.g., *World Book Encyclopedia*), covering a broad range of topics, or subject-specific (e.g., *Encyclopedia of Psychology*). Subject-specific encyclopedias contain detailed articles related to particular fields of study and are written by experts in that field.

Encyclopedias can be good starting points for research. Topics are arranged in alphabetical order and presented in short to medium-length essays. The articles sometimes include illustrations or other visual materials and may reference additional articles or suggest related topics of interest. Encyclopedias may also supply keywords to help you narrow or broaden your search. Online encyclopedias can be accessed without charge or for a subscription fee.

Much of the information in encyclopedias, such as historical facts, does not change. Other information, such as medical interventions and technical data, does change and requires frequent updating. To accommodate changes such as these, many encyclopedia publishers issue yearbooks, which are annual publications documenting recent changes and updates to information.

Examples of general encyclopedias:

- *World Book Encyclopedia*
- *The Encyclopaedia Britannica*

- *The Encyclopedia Americana*
- *The New Lincoln Library Encyclopedia*

Examples of subject-specific encyclopedias:

- *World Book Encyclopedia of People and Places*
- *Famous First Facts, International Edition: A Record of First Happenings, Discoveries, and Inventions in World History*
- *The Encyclopedia of Adoption*
- *U.X.L. Encyclopedia of Biomes*
- *The International Encyclopedia of Adult Education*
- *Advertising Age Encyclopedia of Advertising*
- *The Encyclopedia of Flight*
- *The Encyclopedia of Human Emotions*

2

Dictionaries

A dictionary is an alphabetical listing of words, used to find a word or topic's meaning, spelling, and pronunciation. Dictionaries also include information on parts of speech or word form and word origin. Some dictionaries are general in nature and are useful for basic writing tasks. Others, such as medical dictionaries or slang dictionaries, are specific to a field of study or topic area. These provide more detailed information similar to that found in an encyclopedia and often include illustrations and other reference-type information.

Numerous dictionaries are available on the Internet without charge or accessible through downloadable mobile apps. Examples of general dictionaries:

- *The Oxford English Dictionary*
- *The American Heritage Dictionary*
- *Merriam-Webster's Collegiate Dictionary*
- *The World Book Dictionary*
- *The Random House Dictionary of the English Language*
- *Collins English Dictionary*

Examples of specific dictionaries:

- *The New Dictionary of Cultural Literacy*
- *The Dictionary of Accounting Terms*

- *The Diabetes Dictionary*
- *The Cambridge Aerospace Dictionary*
- *The Historical Dictionary of Afghanistan*
- *The Agriculture Dictionary*
- *Webster's Biographical Dictionary*
- *Webster's Geographical Dictionary*

Directories

A directory is a collection of data organized in a way that allows users to access the information easily. Directories can be alphabetical listings of people, organizations, companies, or institutions. They include addresses, telephone and fax numbers, and other pertinent information. Organizational directories contain member information, as well as dates and information for conferences and publications. Many directories are available online with search features that allow the information to be located easily.

Examples of directories commonly used in research:

- *College Blue Book*
- *Biographical Directory of the United States Congress*
- *Bowker's News Media Directory*
- *Martindale-Hubbell Law Directory*
- *Directory of Physicians in the United States*
- *Writer's Market*
- *Sports Market Place Directory*
- *U.S. Government Manual*

Almanacs

An almanac is a publication that provides statistics, lists, figures, tables, and specific facts in a variety of areas. Almanacs typically are published on an annual or other regular basis. They can be general or subject-specific. You can use almanacs during research to find and compare current or historical information and statistics. Often, this information is in table form for ease of use. Some online almanacs can be accessed without charge and others for a subscription fee.

Examples of general almanacs:

- *The World Almanac and Book of Facts*
- *The Encyclopedia Britannica Almanac*
- *Whitaker's Almanack*
- *Information Please*

Examples of subject-specific almanacs:

- *The African American Almanac*
- *Days to Celebrate: A Full Year of Poetry, People, Holidays, History, Fascinating Facts, and More*
- *Farmer's Almanac*
- *Poor Richard's Almanac*
- *Peterson's College & University Almanac*
- *U.S. Immigration & Migration Almanac*
- *Almanac of American Education*
- *U.X.L. Hispanic American Almanac*
- *Plunkett's Automobile Industry Almanac*
- *Information Please Business Almanac*
- *Sports Illustrated Almanac*

Atlases

An atlas is a collection of geographical and historical information. Atlases incorporate maps, charts, descriptions, tables, demographic information, natural resources statistics, and data on the physical features of geographical areas. You can use atlases to locate places around the world and in outer space, as well as to gather information about the demographics of a region, the physical features of a region, or distances between locations. Because the world is dynamic and political boundaries change, you must ensure that the information is the most current available.

Examples of atlases:

- *World Book Atlas*
- *National Geographic Atlas of the World*
- *Atlas of the World* (Oxford University Press)
- *Oxford New Concise World Atlas*

2

- *Collins World Atlas Gazetteer*
- *Atlas of World Affairs*
- *The Kingfisher Student Atlas*
- *Rand McNally Commercial Atlas & Marketing Guide*
- *Color Atlas of Low Back Pain*
- *Scholastic Atlas of Space*
- *Atlas of the Universe*

Indexes

An index is an alphabetical list, usually at the end of a single-volume reference work or nonfiction book, that can be used to find information within that source. In multivolume reference books, indexes are usually compiled in a separate volume and may also be subject-specific.

Another type of index, the periodical index, is a cumulative list of articles from periodicals. Contents are arranged alphabetically by author, title, or subject. An index entry is called a citation. Each citation in a periodical index contains information about the article, including the author, article title, and the name, volume, issue, and page numbers of the periodical in which the article is published. Periodical indexes may be general, specific to a topic area, or may combine a group of related disciplines. More information about how to use periodical indexes will be discussed in the How Do You Find and Access Information chapter.

Examples of indexes that may be useful in research:

- *Reader's Guide to Periodical Literature*
- *Children's Magazine Guide*
- *Wilson Humanities Index*
- *Education Index*
- *Social Science Index*
- *Art Index*
- *Music Index*
- *Alternative Press Index*
- *Business Periodical Index*
- *Book Review Digest*

Other Common Reference Sources

Often called ready reference sources, these materials usually are kept at or near the reference desk in a library because of their frequent use. In addition to the reference tools mentioned previously, other common ready reference sources include concordances, handbooks, thesauruses, manuals, and style manuals.

Concordance: An alphabetical list of the most pertinent words in a given text and a notation of where they might be found within that text. Concordances are used for in-depth study of a work or collection.

Examples of concordances:

- *A Concordance to Beowulf*
- *A Concordance of the Collected Poems of James Joyce*
- *Strong's Exhaustive Concordance of the Bible*

Handbook: A resource that provides concise data, usually in table or chart form, on a specialized subject area. A handbook is a useful reference for finding current statistics, procedures, instructions, or specific information on a topic.

Examples of handbooks:

- *Handbook of Recreational Games*
- *Boy Scout Handbook*
- *Brownie Girl Scout Handbook*
- *Young Person's Career Skills Handbook*
- *Handbook of Photography*

Thesaurus: A collection of synonyms, near-synonyms, antonyms (word opposites), phrases, and slang terms for words. The two main types of thesaurus are: (1) a Roget-type, which uses a categorization system, and (2) an A–Z type, which lists headwords alphabetically. In a Roget-type thesaurus, the user first looks up the word in the index.

PUT IT TO USE Look at the word before and the word after each category to ensure that you have reviewed all the possible similar entries. Also, look at all parts of speech. You might see another word with a different part of speech that will broaden your word search.

2

The index lists the meanings under each word, and a page number next to each meaning. Then the user goes to that page to find synonyms, antonyms, and other information pertaining to the word.

In the A–Z listing type of thesaurus, each headword (typically bolded) is listed with its parts of speech (verb, noun, adjective, adverb, etc.) and a concise definition. Users will have to consult a dictionary for a more extensive definition. Synonyms are listed under the headword. Most words have several meanings. The words listed together under a headword share at least one meaning with the headword. Usually, the first words listed reflect the most common meanings of the word.

PUT IT TO USE Different words have different connotations, or implied meanings. Be sure you understand the word and its connotation before using it, or you might be saying something you did not intend to say.

A typical thesaurus has synonyms for thousands of words, and may help you find new words to express an idea for which you want to find a different or an opposite word. If you use a thesaurus for this purpose, keep in mind that many words are not directly interchangeable. A thesaurus and a dictionary used together will ensure that you are using the correct word.

Examples of thesauruses:

- *Random House Roget's College Thesaurus*
- *The Thinker's Thesaurus: Sophisticated Alternatives to Common Words*
- *Roget's Descriptive Word Finder*
- *American Heritage Thesaurus for Learners of English*

Style manual: A source that provides guidelines for writing mechanics and documentation format for research papers and theses. Style manuals are updated continually to keep current with new forms of information. For example, style guides provide standard formats for references and resource citations. As information sources develop and are referenced in scholarly works, the guides must be updated so writers can reference their sources according to the guide. Different styles of citing information sources will be discussed in the Legal and Ethical Issues Related to Information chapter.

Examples of style manuals:

- *The Chicago Manual of Style*
- *New York Times Manual of Style and Usage*
- *MLA (Modern Language Association) Style Manual and Guide to Scholarly Publishing*
- *Publication Manual of the American Psychological Association (APA)*
- *Elements of Style*

2

PERIODICALS

A periodical is published on a regular or recurring basis—daily, weekly, monthly, bimonthly, quarterly, or annually. Among periodicals are scholarly journals, popular magazines, trade publications, and newspapers. Periodicals can be issued in print, microform, and electronic formats.

Because periodicals are published frequently, they are expected to provide up-to-date information on a topic. The different types of periodicals and the uses of each are summarized next. Evaluation of periodicals is discussed in the Evaluating Information chapter.

Scholarly Journals

A scholarly journal is typically published by an educational institution or a professional association. The main goal of a scholarly journal is to disseminate information to professionals and researchers in the field in a timely manner. They are often peer-reviewed—sometimes termed refereed—which means that the content of the journal has been read with scrutiny and accepted by knowledgeable reviewers who work in the field or area discussed in the article. Scholarly journals present reports of original research, experiments, or studies, as well as commentaries, discussions on current issues or events, examinations or analyses of specific topic areas, and reviews of scholarly books or other media in the field of study.

A few examples of the many hundreds of scholarly journals:

- *Journal of the American Medical Association (JAMA)*
- *Harvard Law Review*
- *American Journal of Occupational Therapy (AJOT)*

- *The Journal of American Culture*
- *The Journal of Individual Society*
- *Community College Journal*
- *Journal of Sport Management*
- *Journal of Environmental Engineering*
- *School Library Journal*

Popular Magazines

A popular magazine provides information on topics of interest to the general public, including (but certainly not limited to) news, entertainment, lifestyle, popular culture, leisure reading, parenting, home, science and nature, self-improvement, and do-it-yourself projects. Although some of these magazines provide well-researched and documented information, many do not. The articles are typically short, lacking references or substantive information, often providing information of a sensational nature, and containing advertisements.

A few examples of the many hundreds of popular magazines:

- *Good Housekeeping*
- *Redbook*
- *Vanity Fair*
- *People*
- *Time*
- *Newsweek*
- *U.S. News & World Report*
- *Vogue*
- *Sports Illustrated*
- *Popular Mechanics*

Trade Publications

A trade publication is a periodical intended for a specific industry or business, usually published by an association tied to the trade. The authors of articles in trade publications are usually practitioners or professionals in a specific field. The goal of these articles is to inform others in the industry. Trade publications typically contain articles that provide applied information versus research.

A few examples of the many hundreds of trade publications:

- *Women's Wear Daily*
- *Furniture World*
- *Hoard's Dairyman*
- *Aramco World*
- *Advertising Age*
- *Stores & Retail Spaces*
- *Chain Store Age*
- *Bobbin*
- *Booklist*

Newspapers

Newspapers are of a local, regional, national, or international venue and are general or topic-specific. They usually cover current news and events and come in both a paper and online format. As print readership is steadily declining, however, the trend has been for more and more students and professionals to access them exclusively online.

A few examples of the many hundreds of newspapers:

- *New York Times*
- *Boston Globe*
- *USA Today*
- *Kansas City Star*
- *St. Louis Post Dispatch*
- *Wall Street Journal*
- *Al Jazeera*

MULTIMEDIA

Information can be in a form other than print or electronic. Many libraries house or have access to a variety of graphic, audio, video, and film media sources of information. Among these are maps, CD-ROMs, DVDs, Blu-Rays, 16-mm films, audio files, vinyl records, and so forth. Each library or library system has access to various media and may be able to borrow a desired media resource from another library using the interlibrary loan system.

Self-Assessment Questions

- What industry-specific periodicals are appropriate for your profession or field of study?
- What types of information contained in periodicals would you expect to change often?

INFORMATION RETRIEVAL SYSTEMS

Information retrieval systems allow access to electronic resources and information. Electronic resources include online catalogs, databases, indexes, abstracts, and full-text articles in electronic journals, reference sources, and e-books that are stored in an electronic format and accessed by computer or smart devices.

ONLINE PUBLIC ACCESS CATALOG (OPAC)

A library catalog is a register of all bibliographic items in a specific library or library system. A bibliographic item is any piece of information or information resource that is a library material. In the past, researchers located library holdings by searching a card catalog—a file cabinet containing individual cards with bibliographic information about specific items in the library. Since the mid-1980s, the physical card catalog has been replaced in most places with a computerized catalog called an OPAC.

An OPAC is a computerized online catalog of all the materials held in a library and can be searched quickly and efficiently using a computer. OPACs can be searched using author, title, subject, call number, or keyword. The purpose of cataloging library resources is to help the library patron find the resource, to show what the library has available, and to provide enough information for the user to make a decision about selecting the resource. Many libraries have also made their OPACs accessible via the Internet. These OPACs are most often Windows-based and, to simplify the search, use pull-down menus, pop-up windows, dialog boxes, mouse operations, and graphical user interface components.

Library cataloging follows established cataloging rules that have been designed to ensure consistent cataloging of library materials. Most cataloging rules are based on the International Standard Bibliographic Description (ISBD), produced by the International Federation of Library Associations (IFLA).

DATABASES

A database is a collection of digitized information organized for simplified, fast searching and retrieval. Databases are updated regularly and contain bibliographic citations or references for periodicals, books, reports, and other publications. Full-text databases contain these citations, as well as the full text of the periodical, book, or report. A database may be general or subject-specific.

Vendors of databases are called aggregators. An aggregated service simultaneously accesses information from several databases. Examples of aggregators are Gale, EBSCOhost, and ProQuest. Libraries subscribe to these resources to make information readily available to their staffs and library users. Electronic formats allow convenient searching of the resource, using techniques that narrow the search to pinpoint the exact data needed.

Examples of databases:

- *PsycINFO:* A database of more than three million records of peer-reviewed literature in the behavioral sciences and mental health areas.
- *Academic Search Premier:* A database that includes both scholarly and peer-reviewed journals dating back to 1975.
- *Business Source Premiere:* A database that indexes journals related to the many areas of business.

THE INTERNET

The Internet is a high-speed electronic network, sometimes called the "information superhighway," that connects millions of computers, tablets, smartphones, and other web-enabled devices around the world, allowing users to communicate through email, messaging, file transfers, social media, and in many other ways. This network is connected by fiber optics, telephone lines, cables, and communications satellites. A rich source of information, the Internet allows users to access a limitless amount of data if they have the skills to find this information.

The Internet is a massive information-retrieval system. The World Wide Web is an international network of Internet servers that allows access to documents written in HTML (hypertext markup language) and provides links to other documents, graphic files, audio files, video files, and many other forms of information. This means that you can move from one resource to another by clicking on links within a resource. Note that "Internet" is not

2

synonymous with "World Wide Web." The World Wide Web is something that is available via the Internet, as are email and other Internet services. Consider the World Wide Web to be a read–write information space for Internet resources such as images, text, videos, and other media.

A website is made up of a collection of webpages that are stored in a single folder or within related subfolders of a web server. A webpage is an electronic resource on the World Wide Web that is assigned a unique Internet address called a uniform resource locator (URL). It is displayed using a web browser such as Google Chrome. Webpages can contain numerous types of information including text and graphics, audio and video, interactive multimedia, applets (subprograms that run inside the page), links, and downloadable files.

In some cases, the user has to download additional software modules, called plug-ins, and install them on the computer to run interactive elements and applets or to display specialized types of data. Hundreds of plug-ins are available on the Internet, downloadable free of charge. Most specialized software applications for graphics, video, and animation have their own plug-ins that are required to view their content. In most cases, the webpage will have a link and instructions on how to locate and download the needed plug-ins.

Examples of plug-ins for viewing elements and specialized plug-ins for webpages:

- *Adobe Flash Player:* runs .swf animation movies and YouTube videos.
- *Apple QuickTime:* enables viewing of video, sound, animation, text, graphics, and so forth.
- *Acrobat Reader:* allows viewing of .pdf files.
- *Java Virtual Machine:* runs Java applets.
- *Microsoft Silverlight:* runs rich media, databases, and interactive webpages.
- *RealMedia:* enables viewing of video, sound, animation, and graphics including streaming audio and video.
- *Adblock Plus:* blocks banner ads, pop ups, and any image source URLs for multiple browsers.

Webpages also contain content that cannot be seen in a browser. For example, a webpage contains scripts (often JavaScript) that add functionality to the page. When you roll the mouse over a place on a page and additional text appears, you are seeing the results of JavaScript. Another unseen element on a webpage is a Cascading Style Sheet, which tells how the page is to be formatted. Meta tags provide hidden information about the page itself, providing information to search engines to help in categorizing the page for search purposes.

A home page is the main or first screen of a website, with links to other pages on the site. This first page also is called an index page and may be described that way in the webpage's address ending in index .html, or something similar. Many college and university libraries have home pages with links to various research resources and their OPAC. Many webpages include a navigation bar with links to other pages on the website, or sometimes to entirely different websites. Navigation bars can be horizontal or vertical, depending upon the website design. Typically, the navigation bar is seen on all pages of the website to make it easy to jump from one area to another. If you get to a page that does not have the navigation bar, you can simply click your browser's back button to go back to the page showing the navigation bar. The back button takes you, in order, to the pages visited previously.

Common links on the navigation bar are *About* (provides information about the sponsor of the website), *Home* (takes you to the home page of the site), *Contact Us* (provides contact information), and *Resources* (provides additional resources or external links). Additional links on the navigation bar may be to company departments, products and services, certificates, publications, and other relevant pages, depending on the purpose and design of the site.

Web Browsers

Although you can view most webpages with any software application that can read text documents, to view a webpage as it is intended and to access all of the page's functionality, you must use software called a web browser. The browser interprets the Internet files and puts them in a readable format. There are many different web browsers with different capabilities. Even different versions of the same web browser have different capabilities.

Examples of commonly used browsers:

- *Google Chrome*
- *Mozilla Firefox*

- *Internet Explorer*
- *Microsoft Edge*
- *Opera*
- *Safari*

2

Search Engines

Because there are millions of Internet sites, we must have an efficient way to search for the information and sites we need. Search engines use computer software that makes the World Wide Web searchable through keywords or phrases. Search results may be listed by relevancy, by currency, or by some other method. The Internet has many different search engines that can be used to find information, but because each search engine allows searching through only those files in its specific database, using only one search engine provides only a small portion of the available sites on the Internet. To find a more complete list of Internet sites, meta-search engines search multiple individual search engines simultaneously. For extensive information, ratings, and tips on using search engines effectively, go to SearchEngineWatch on the Internet.

Examples of commonly used search engines:

- Google
- Bing
- Yahoo! Search
- Ask
- AOL Search

Critical Thinking Questions

- How do online search engines work?
- How might different search engines affect the results of a search? (This might take some research!)
- Is the large number of results from an Internet search a bad thing? Why or why not?
- Under what circumstances might you want to limit the number of results you receive?

PUT IT TO USE Keep in mind that when you are using a search engine, you are not searching the entire Internet; you are searching a portion of it.

Internet Information Resources

As stated earlier, many resources available in a physical library are now available on the Internet via virtual libraries, subject directories, and individual websites. Many of the resources are free, and others are fee-based or subscription services. Some of the more useful Internet information sources are explored in more depth here.

Internet Subject Directories

An important tool on the Internet is a subject directory: A collection of links to a large number of Internet resources, typically organized by topic area. Commercial subject directories are general in nature and are much less selective. Academic and professional directories are usually maintained by experts and cater to professionals who need credible information.

Examples of Internet subject directories:

- INFOMINE (infomine.ucr.edu)
- The Internet Public Library (www.ipl.org)

Online Reference Resources

Information-literate individuals can easily access online reference resources such as dictionaries, thesauruses, encyclopedias, almanacs, handbooks, directories, and so forth via the Internet. Fee structures for these resources vary from no charge to an annual or monthly subscription charge. Some sites are free but require a registration, and others allow free use of basic services while charging a fee for more advanced or expanded services.

Examples of useful reference resources on the Internet:

- Refdesk (www.refdesk.com)
- Questia (www.questia.com)
- Merriam-Webster Online (www.m-w.com)
- Encyclopedia.com (www.encyclopedia.com)
- Occupational Outlook Handbook (www.bls.gov/ooh)

PUT IT TO USE Though it is a convenient source of information, Wikipedia should not be used for academic research. Wikipedia is written and edited by its readers and sometimes contains misinformation, and it is not considered an authoritative source. You should look to other online sources that contain more consistent and refereed information.

2

Online Periodicals

As discussed earlier in the chapter, a single library does not subscribe to every available periodical. An alternative to using the library's periodicals is to find a full-text version of the article online. The general procedure to search for full-text articles is basically the same as that for a physical library. An online periodical index enables users to find the needed citation information. In many cases, the actual full-text article can be accessed directly from the citation. Some full-text articles are available free, and others must be purchased. Many online libraries and subject directories also link to periodical indexes and to the articles themselves.

Examples of periodical sites on the Internet:

- PubMed Central (http://www.ncbi.nlm.nih.gov/pmc/)
- HighBeam (www.highbeam.com)
- NewsLink (newslink.org)
- FindArticles (www.findarticles.com)

Web Portals

A web portal, sometimes called a gateway, is a site on the Internet that provides links to many different kinds of information. Some portals are general in nature, and others provide links to information in a specific topic area, such as business, computers, law, or medicine. On a web portal, you can find industry-related information, products, news, periodicals, organizations, chat rooms, people finders, and almost anything else related to the industry and found on the Internet. Some web portals are maintained by Internet service providers (ISPs), and others are maintained by states, professional organizations, or special interest groups. There are hundreds, if not thousands, of web portals for almost every industry.

Examples of general-use web portals available on the Internet include:

- AOL (www.aol.com)
- About (www.about.com)
- USA.gov (www.usa.gov)

Examples of web portals that may be relevant to your field of study include:

Business

- Forbes (www.forbes.com)
- Financial Web (http://www.finweb.com/)
- Market Watch (http://www.marketwatch.com/)

Legal Studies

- Jurist (http://www.jurist.org/)
- Guide to Law Online (http://www.loc.gov/law/help/guide.php)
- MERLOT Criminal Justice (https://www.merlot.org/merlot/CriminalJustice.htm)

Healthcare

- WebMD (http://www.webmd.com/)
- Science.gov (http://www.science.gov/)
- Nurse Portal (http://www.nurseportal.net/)

Education

- abcteach (http://www.abcteach.com/)
- Apples for the Teacher (http://www.apples4theteacher.com/)
- A to Z Teacher (http://atozteacherstuff.com/)

SMARTPHONE APPS

In recent years, on-the-go learning has grown in popularity due to the many online resources that can be accessed using smartphones. In fact, some colleges and universities have begun releasing their own mobile education apps. Several commonly used apps for college students are listed as follows:

- Evernote—record voice memos, to-do-lists, and notes
- EasyBib—build and manage cited works
- iHomework—organize course schedule, appointments, homework, and more
- Trello—organize group projects and manage tasks

- Dropbox—keep videos, audio, papers, and other important files on your phone
- Zite—personalized magazine used to control your incoming news

2

PROFESSIONAL AND TRADE ORGANIZATIONS

Professional and trade organizations are groups of professionals who have similar interests or positions. These organizations are excellent sources for current information in an industry, for trends and current practices, for licensure and certification information, and for networking with other professionals who have similar interests. Most organizations have some kind of online presence and offer excellent and credible information on their websites. Information-literate individuals can stay current in their field by participating in professional organizations and by reviewing these websites regularly. A good starting place to find appropriate professional organization websites is with Google's directory listing for professional organizations.

Examples of professional organizations:

- The American Occupational Therapy Association (www.aota.org)
- Association of Information Technology Professionals (www.aitp.org)
- Computer Technology Industry Association (CompTIA) (www.comptia.org)
- American Health Information Management Association (AHIMA) (www.ahima.org)
- American Association of Medical Assistants (AAMA) (www.aama-ntl.org)

Self-Assessment Questions

- What professional organizations are appropriate for your field?
- What information do these organizations maintain on their websites?

CHAPTER SUMMARY

This chapter provided you with strategies for creating main and focused research questions and clarified the purposes of each. After establishing your research questions, you learned several information sources and how to access each.

POINTS TO KEEP IN MIND

- Main and focused research questions are important in directing your research and organizing your research information effectively.
- Main research questions should be specific and answered by verifiable facts.
- Focused research questions should direct your research and organize your information search strategies.
- Primary information sources are those that have not been altered or interpreted and are preferred for research.
- If you use secondary resources, it is best to find and reference the primary source as well as the secondary source.
- Know the resources that are best suited to answering your research question as well as how to select and access them.

apply it

Activity #1: Resource Exploration

STEP 1: Review your library resources, consult with the reference librarian at your local library or school library, and search the Internet to complete the Resource Table for your field of study.

STEP 2: Continue to add to the list as you find additional resources, and keep this table electronically for reference as you conduct research and locate additional resources.

Resource Table

Resource Type	Resource Name	Resource Location and Access Instructions	Description
Primary Information Sources			
Secondary Information Sources			
Nonfiction Books			
General Encyclopedias			
Subject-Specific Encyclopedias			

continued

2

General Dictionaries			
Subject-Specific Dictionaries			
Directories			
Almanacs			
Atlases			
Indexes			
Concordances			
Handbooks			
Thesauruses			
Manuals			
Scholarly Journals			
Popular Magazines			
Trade Publications			
Databases			

Activity #2: Database Exploration

STEP 1: Using your library's resources, explore the databases that are available to you. Usually these include a brief description of the database. Some libraries list databases in alphabetical order and by subject covered.

STEP 2: Thinking of your field of study, list the specific databases that are appropriate for your research.

Activity #3: Search Engine Comparison

STEP 1: Do a search for a limited topic of your choice using a search engine, and then do the same search using a meta-search engine.

STEP 2: Compare and contrast the results. What is the difference in the number of results of your search? What is the difference in the type of results or sites that are returned?

STEP 3: Note which search engine(s) best meets your needs.

Activity #4: Internet Resource Exploration

STEP 1: Explore the Internet to complete the Internet Resource Table for your field of study.

STEP 2: Continue to add to the list as you find additional resources, and keep this table electronically for reference as you conduct research.

Internet Resource Table

Resource Type	Resource Name	Resource URL and Access Instructions	Description
Web Browsers			
Common Plug-ins for Your Browser			
Search Engines			
Internet Subject Directories			
Online Reference Resources			
Online Periodicals			
Web Portals			
Professional and Trade Organizations			

2

SUGGESTED ITEMS FOR LEARNING PORTFOLIO

Refer to the "How to Use This Book" section at the beginning of this textbook for more information on learning portfolios.

- Resource Table
- Database Exploration List
- Comparison of Search Engine Report

REFERENCES

Library of Congress. (n.d.). *Primary Source Analysis Tool.* Retrieved June 14, 2013, from http://www.loc.gov/teachers/primary-source-analysis-tool/

Raimes, A. and Miller-Cochran, S. (2013). *Keys for Writers (7/e).* Boston, MA: Wadsworth, Cengage Learning.

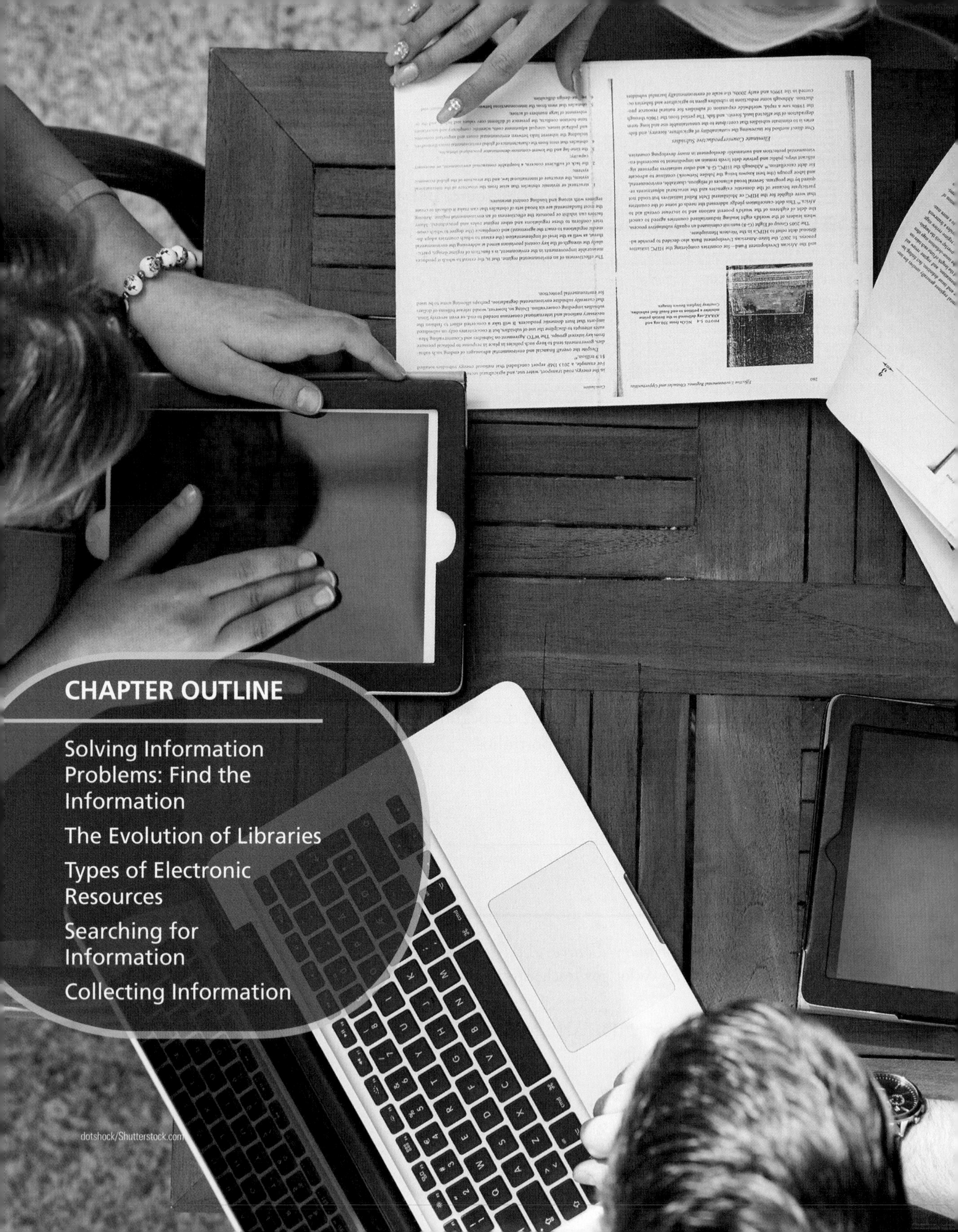

CHAPTER OUTLINE

- Solving Information Problems: Find the Information
- The Evolution of Libraries
- Types of Electronic Resources
- Searching for Information
- Collecting Information

dotshock/Shutterstock.com

How Do You Find and Access Information?

LEARNING OBJECTIVES

By the end of this chapter, you will be able to:

- Use several techniques to search for relevant information efficiently.
- Identify several common sources for information.
- Use library resources to find and access information.
- Use electronic resources to find and access information.
- Explain the importance of having a method for collecting information.

BE IN THE KNOW

The Library of Congress

The Library of Congress is the nation's oldest federal cultural institution and serves as the research arm of Congress. It is also the largest library in the world, with more than 162 million items on approximately 838 miles of bookshelves. The collections include more than 38.6 million books and other print materials, over 3.6 million audio materials, 14.2 million photographs, 5.6 million maps, 7.2 million pieces of sheet music, and 70.3 million manuscripts.

"The Library of Congress occupies three buildings on Capitol Hill. The Thomas Jefferson Building (1897) is the original separate Library of Congress building. (The Library began in 1800 inside the U.S. Capitol.) The John Adams Building was built in 1938, and the James Madison Memorial Building was completed in 1981" (Library of Congress, n.d. [a]).

Major exhibitions of the library are also available online, as are selected prints and photographs, historic films, and political speeches. Find the Library of Congress Online Catalog at catalog2.loc.gov. You can search these records by keyword or browse by authors/creators, subjects, name/titles, uniform titles, and call numbers. Browse lists also include searching aids such cross-references and scope notes (Library of Congress, n.d. [b]).

Whether you visit in person or online, the Library of Congress is a national treasure and an invaluable reference tool. Use it!

SOLVING INFORMATION PROBLEMS: FIND THE INFORMATION

Even with an effective main research question and several focused research questions that serve to narrow the research scope sufficiently, finding the right information can still be a daunting task. To complete Step 2: Find the Information, as shown in Figure 3-1, you first must understand how libraries have adapted to changes in technology, how they are organized, how the materials in libraries and information

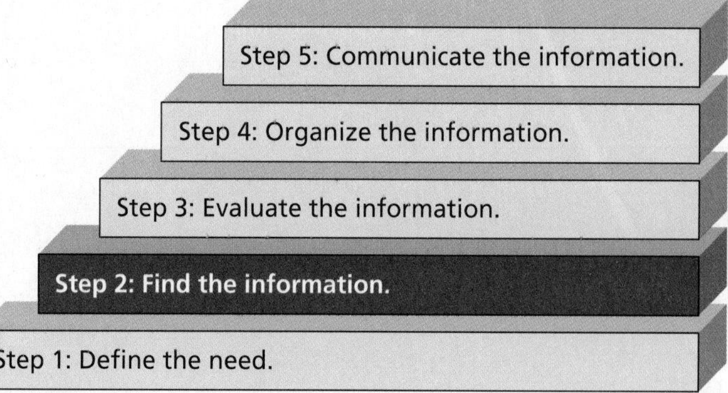

Figure 3-1 Research Process Step 2: Find the Information
The second step of any research project should be to efficiently find the information.

on the Internet are cataloged and referenced, and how to access and efficiently use these reference tools.

THE EVOLUTION OF LIBRARIES

The use of libraries dates back to ancient times. Throughout their existence, libraries have always managed to remain adaptable to the needs of their users. This is no more evident than it is today.

The availability of and access to information has changed dramatically with the advent of the Internet and other communication avenues over the past 20 to 30 years, and will continue on. During this time, libraries have had to embrace these new technologies in order to meet the changing needs of their users. Libraries were not the inventors of these communication avenues, but they were early adopters of them. Libraries sensed the shifting needs of their audience and thus embraced how they could find, evaluate, and communicate information to users in new and meaningful ways to solve information problems, whether that be for a research paper, for finding a job, or to answer personal questions about taxes or medical issues, to name a few. Given the proliferation of new technologies as tools for research, many libraries are now using the term media center or media center library instead. A media center is simply a library, usually in a school, that contains and encourages the use of audiovisual media and associated equipment, as well as books, periodicals, and the like (Dictionary.com, 2016).

Today, libraries fill an even greater role in the community by becoming collaborators with those they serve. Libraries are no longer seen as just loaners of books, but instead they are heralded as epicenters for providing a wide variety of services that help to fulfill a community's needs. Libraries and librarians are continually working to understand how patrons use information, and thus rely on input and feedback from those very users to improve their "product" of being information providers.

CRITICAL THINKING QUESTIONS

- How do you see libraries collaborating within their communities?
- How has the collaboration extended beyond the physical walls of the library?

HOW LIBRARIES ARE ORGANIZED

Whether it is a public, national, school, academic, or special library (such as a law library, medical library, or museum library), all libraries organize their holdings using a library catalog, which is a log or register of all the items in the library. Materials in a library are referred to as

3

bibliographic items. A library item can be any piece of information, such as a book, a graphic, a map, a DVD, a Blu-ray, an audio file, a computer file, and so on. Before the computer came into extensive use in the 1980s, libraries physically documented their library catalog using a card catalog. Pre-computer card catalogs were large sets of physical file cabinets holding a catalog record (small index cards) containing each library item's relevant information. Information on the catalog record included the call number, author, title, edition, publisher, brief physical description of the item, notes about the item's content, and a valid Library of Congress subject heading assigned to the item. The file cabinets were organized to enable searching using different types of information, such as by author, title, or subject.

Nearly all physical card catalogs have been replaced by a convenient computer system—the online public access catalog (OPAC). Although some libraries still retain their card catalogs, few libraries update these physical references. You might see a sign posted stating the last year the card catalog was updated. More current information would then reside on the OPAC. Some libraries have removed their card catalogs altogether to make space for additional book stacks or technology.

We discussed OPACs in depth in the Determining the Information You Need chapter. The following is a review of important points to keep in mind.

OPACs catalog the holdings of a specific library or library system. Each library or library system has access to various resources. Some libraries house information pertaining to a specific area, such as medicine or law. In other libraries the collection is designed for the general public. Educational libraries on college and university campuses contain holdings for both the general public and the school's specific programs of study and research.

OPACs do not catalog information within a specific library holding. In many cases, libraries lend materials to patrons of a different library through the interlibrary loan system. OPACs, including those that are web-based, do not catalog all holdings everywhere, only holdings for that specific library or library system.

OPACs do not catalog all of the items in a library. Many libraries store informational items that are not cataloged. These items might include local historical documents, old phone books, school yearbooks, folders of newspaper clippings, manuscripts, photographs, map collections, pamphlets, and so forth. If you are looking for these kinds of items, or others that you can't find in the catalog, ask the reference librarian.

OPACs allow for searching using several criteria. These criteria include author of the work, title of the work, official designated subject heading, and keywords.

Many other resources are available outside a library or library system on the Internet. In addition to OPACs, which make searching for a library's resources convenient and efficient, many valuable information sources can be accessed via the Internet. Information-literate individuals understand both library and nonlibrary resources and how to locate and access these resources efficiently.

3

Throughout the course of your education or career, you have likely used many print resources such as books and periodicals. Libraries have many nonprint materials as well. Nonprint materials are items that are published in any format other than paper and may or may not be cataloged in the OPAC. To use any of these items, ask the reference librarian for help.

Nonprint Resources Commonly Found in a Library	
Computer files	Blu-ray
Sound recordings	CD-ROMs
Visual materials	Cassette tapes
Computer disks	Video tapes (videocassettes)
Video discs	Laser discs
DVDs	Vinyl records
Models	Motion pictures (film reels)
Slides	Photographs
Kits	Microform

USING DIGITAL LIBRARIES

In addition to OPACs, many schools and organizations are creating and using digital (or online) libraries. This takes the online experience from a simple search (like Google) to accessing information and books that are stored online. Some library sites may require you to establish a username and password before granting access. Other sites may charge a small fee to access their information.

3

Digital libraries have many advantages over their traditional brick-and-mortar counterparts. These advantages include:

- **Convenient hours.** Unlike a conventional library, a digital library may be accessed 24/7/365.
- **Access from anywhere.** As long as you are logged on to a computer with Internet access and know the library's URL, you can be physically located anywhere in the world and tap into the library's resources. In addition, many smartphone apps have been developed that provide mobile access to select library resources. For example, the Library of Congress has several apps available at https://www.loc.gov/apps/.
- **Multiple users.** Digital libraries can accommodate multiple users reviewing the same information at the same time.
- **Length of time the book can be "checked out."** With a traditional library, most books and other resources can only be checked out for a set length of time. With a digital library, there may be a greater, or even no, time limit, and you can retrieve the same information over and over again.
- **Generally no fees.** Conventional libraries will charge a nominal fee per day if a book or resource is not returned by the due date. This, of course, is not the case with a digital library because digital resources are no longer accessible after the due date.
- **Online chat capability.** This is a quick way to get your question answered by the online reference librarian.

There are a few disadvantages to a digital library:

- **The reference librarian may not always be available.** Even though an online chat feature is an advantage of a digital library, the hours of operation may be limited. In the event that the reference librarian is unavailable, you usually have to fill out a form and wait a certain period of time before you receive a response. If you know you are going to need help with your research, it is best to build in additional time to address your reference needs.
- **Not everything is online.** Some materials are only in print form, and therefore will not be available to you online. As technology continues to evolve, this may become less of an issue. But for now, do note that sometimes a walk to the library is in order.

WORKING WITH YOUR LIBRARIAN

One of the greatest resources available to students during their academic career is the school librarian. Librarians offer a wealth of expertise on finding and evaluating information in a digital environment that even the information-literate student may never acquire. Additionally, librarians are tech-savvy and are well schooled on the latest trends of how their users want to receive information. The information-literate learner recognizes that leveraging this additional expertise will aid in success in both the classroom and the workplace.

CRITICAL THINKING QUESTIONS

- Do you think you utilize the librarians at your school as much as you should?
- What researching skills do you think you could learn from your librarians?

3

CASE IN POINT: THE SEARCH FOR RESEARCH

Danielle Watson has been given an assignment to write a research paper for her college history course. Her professor has allowed free choice on the selection of topics. Danielle has learned about using the library and its resources, but this is the first time she has been instructed to write a paper that requires her to put this information to use. For this assignment, the professor stipulates that the students use specific resources, including primary and secondary sources. These required resources include:

- five nonfiction books
- five reference resources
- appropriate indexes
- two general databases
- two subject-specific databases
- four scholarly journals
- three credible websites

- What plan does Danielle have to make to complete the assignment successfully?
- What should Danielle's first step be?
- Whom could Danielle consult as she begins her research?
- What kinds of information sources does Danielle need to begin her research?
- Where can she find these resources?
- How will Danielle search for the information within each resource?
- What information-gathering strategies can be used?

TYPES OF ELECTRONIC RESOURCES

Increasingly, reference materials can be found in electronic (or digital) form. The following items may be available to you through your school's library or perhaps an interlibrary loan system. Consider using any of these electronic sources of information as you conduct research.

E-JOURNALS

Electronic journals, also known as e-journals, are electronic versions of scholarly journals used for research. Oftentimes, e-journals are available via subscription through an Electronic Journals Service (EJS) such as EBSCOhost. Check with your school's library or Learning Resource Center to see if it has such a service available to you.

E-BOOKS

E-books are digitized versions of published books that are readable on a computer, e-reader, or smart phone. Some advantages of e-books include generally lower costs than their printed counterparts, easier and lighter transport, and immediate availability via download.

STREAMING VIDEOS

Streaming videos continue to gain in popularity. There is virtually no end to what one can watch via streaming video, including TV shows, news, sports, movies, and gaming. Popular sites and services include YouTube, Vimeo, Netflix, Amazon Prime, Sling TV, and Hulu.

PODCASTS

Podcasting is the syndication and distribution of digital interactive media files (audio, video, and text) over the Internet. The content contained in a podcast can be virtually anything, from a song, to an educational lecture, to a political debate. There are hundreds of educational podcasts available online. Use a search engine and type in "educational podcasts" to access them. Your school's library may also have access to podcasts.

BLOGS

A blog, shortened from the word weblog, is a publication forum on the Internet where articles (called posts) are placed and where others can read and comment. Posts are usually listed in reverse chronological order, so that the most recent information or comments are seen first.

There are millions and millions of blogs in existence today on every subject imaginable. Blogs on a particular topic you are researching may provide useful information. Use a search engine to access blogs on a specific subject.

GRAPHICS AND IMAGES

Graphics and images can greatly enhance how information is presented. An Internet search of your research topic may yield many representations of your subject. The Organizing Information chapter has additional information about how to organize graphics. Infographics, or information graphics, are a type of graphical representation designed to make data easily understandable at a glance. Their purpose is to communicate a message by simplifying the presentation of large amounts of data. For example, a professional working in business may use infographics, such as bar graphs and pie charts, to convey information at a high level. For students as well as professionals, there are many infographic makers available online. Examples include Piktochart (www.piktochart.com) and Venngage (https://venngage.com).

GOOGLE SCHOLAR

Google Scholar (scholar.google.com) searches a wide variety of scholarly publications from various content providers, including universities, academic publishers, and professional societies. Many campus libraries provide a direct link to Google Scholar from their intranet site.

WIKIS

A wiki is a webpage that can be viewed and modified by anyone with a web browser and access to the Internet. Wikis urge collaboration and contribution by its users. Because *anyone*, expert or not, can place and alter information on a wiki, many schools do not consider information gleaned from a wiki a credible or reliable source. Even Wikipedia, a site that is often consulted by college-age students, has issued the following statement: "It is in the nature of an ever-changing work like Wikipedia that, while some articles are of the highest quality of scholarship, others are admittedly complete rubbish. We are fully aware of what it is and what it isn't. Also, because some articles may contain errors, please do not use Wikipedia to make critical decisions" (Wikipedia, 2016). This is an example of why it is very important to check your school's policy on the use and citation of wiki information prior to starting your research project.

3

Self-Assessment Questions

- What are some types of infographics you would use if you were doing a classroom presentation in a course within your field of study?
- Which social media sites could be useful in an academic or professional setting? How would you use them in terms of research and communication?

SOCIAL MEDIA

The use of social media for academic research is proliferating quickly. As of August 2015, there were over 2.2 billion active users of social media worldwide and of that total, over 1.9 billion people make use of a mobile device to access social media platforms. Facebook, in particular, has had phenomenal growth with approximately half a million users joining daily (Regan, 2015).

The following are some examples of tools and resources that help people find and share information in an educational setting.

- Social bookmarking, news, and social citation tools such as CiteULike, delicious, and Reddit.
- Social networking services including LinkedIn, Facebook, and Academia.edu.
- Blogging and microblogging tools such as Blogger, Tumblr, and Twitter.
- Presentation sharing tools including Scribd, SlideShare, and SlideRocket.
- Audio and video tools such as Flickr, Livestream, and SmugMug.
- Research and writing collaboration tools including Dropbox, Google Docs, and Wetpaint.
- Information management tools, for instance, iGoogle and Netvibes.

- Project management, meeting, and collaboration tools, for example, Basecamp, Skype, and Huddle (Cann, Dimitriou, & Hooley, 2011).

Check your school's policies on the use of social media for academic research before assuming that its use is acceptable.

DEEP WEB AND DARK WEB

In the Determining the Information You Need chapter, you learned that the World Wide Web includes websites that are accessible from search engines, such as Google Chrome and Microsoft Edge. There are areas of the World Wide Web, however, that are not indexed by most commonly used search engines. This part of the web is known as the Deep Web, Deep Net, Invisible Web, or Hidden Web. As the Deep Web includes approximately 96 percent of the information on the Internet, there is a wide array of research materials available.

There is, however, a subset of the Deep Web called the Dark Web that is considered to be a very dangerous place. The Deep Web's anonymity attracts criminal activity ranging from the sale of drugs and weapons to the trading of child pornography and even the hiring of contract killers (Laverty, 2016). This type of activity occurs in the Dark Web, which exists on networks called darknets. It is important to remember that many people use the terms Dark Web and Deep Web interchangeably, but they are not the same. The Deep Web isn't necessarily malicious and can provide useful research material, but the Dark Web contains illegal activity and content that should be avoided.

SEARCHING FOR INFORMATION

As discussed in the Determining the Information You Need chapter, search tools such as OPACs, databases, indexes, and so forth help researchers find information. Understanding basic search techniques is essential to use these tools effectively. The first step in conducting a search for information is to know the types of information available for most library resources, which include the following four pieces of information:

1. Author
2. Title
3. Subject
4. Keyword

Specific strategies for searching using each of these types of information are described in the sections that follow. These strategies will be helpful in developing search statements, also referred to as search strings, which are search engine queries written in a manner that greatly increases the likelihood of the most accurate and relevant information being returned.

AUTHOR SEARCH

An author search is used to locate works by the author. You have to know at least the author's last name. Any additional information, such as the first and middle name or initials, will make your search more efficient by limiting the number of items within your search results. For example, to find writings by James Michener, you could search using any of the following names:

Michener

Michener, J

Michener, James

In many cases, a work is authored by more than one person. If a work has more than one author, use all of the names to limit the search appropriately.

An author may also be an organization, rather than a person. When searching for materials published by an organization, you can search by the organization's name, part of the name, and often the acronym for the organization. For example, if you want to search for materials written or published by the American College of Sports Medicine, you could use any of the following terms to start your search:

American

American College

American College of Sports

American College of Sports Medicine

ACSM

The more accurately you describe the organization by using all of the words in the name, the more relevant your search results will be. For instance, in the earlier example you will have many more unrelated results when you search "American" than you will when you search "American College of Sports Medicine."

TITLE SEARCH

A title search is used to locate specific titles of books, references, periodicals, and other resources. If you know the title or part of the title of the book or material for which you are searching, a title search is appropriate. For example, if you are searching for the book *The Da Vinci Code,* you could use the following search terms to locate the book quickly:

The Da Vinci Code

Da Vinci Code

Da Vinci

Keep in mind that the more accurate and complete the information you use for your search terms, the fewer will be the number of items appearing in your search results. Many books and other materials have Da Vinci in the title. By supplying the full title—*The Da Vinci Code*—you will limit your search results significantly and save time that otherwise would be required to sort through all of the results to find exactly what you want.

PUT IT TO USE Most catalogs ignore the initial articles "A," "An," and "The."

SUBJECT SEARCH

A subject search is used to find materials on a specific topic. Standardized subject headings are assigned by the Library of Congress, and these subject headings are listed in the *Library of Congress Subject Headings (LCSH)* publication. This multivolume set, typically found at the reference desk of the library, provides synonyms for the subject, as well as related terms to narrow or broaden your search. The *LCSH* also provides references that will direct you to the specific subject heading that is used for a general topic.

For example, if you are searching for "farming," the Library of Congress subject information would state "see Agriculture," directing you to search under the general topic of "Agriculture." If you were to search for "musicians," you would be directed to use a more specific category related to that term. The *LCSH* listing might provide the information, "see Jazz Musicians" or "see American Musicians."

In addition, the *LCSH* organizes large subjects logically into categories directing you to the correct subject listing. An author can be a subject as well as the author of a work. The more information you provide, the more accurate the search results will be. To find items *about* an author, you would treat the author as a subject and search by the author's last name, as in:

Shakespeare, William
Dickinson, Emily
Thoreau, Henry David

Critical Thinking Question

- What do you think the results would be if you were to use just the term "Brown" as the subject search term, without "Larry," in your search for information about Larry Brown, a contemporary author?

An examination of the *LCSH* information will provide insight into how the headings are used. Referring to Figure 3-2, the subject for this entry is "Mental Illness." The listing provides a brief description of the kinds of information that might be found under the "Mental Illness" subject, then gives several abbreviations to help you find additional subject headings that might be more appropriate for your search.

LCSH abbreviations include the following:

- *May Subd Geog:* This notation indicates that the subject may be geographically subdivided, meaning that other subject listings may be related more closely to your specific search subject. The hyphens indicate a subdivision, for example, Mental Illness-Australia.

- *UF:* This abbreviation denotes *unauthorized headings.* The common subjects listed here are not used in the *LCSH* subject list, and you will waste your time using these search terms to look for your resources. In the example of "Mental Illness" in Figure 3-2, the common terms of "Diseases, Mental," "Madness," "Mental disorders," and "Mental diseases" would not be effective search terms.
- *BT:* This abbreviation stands for *broader topic*, a more general topic. This notation gives subject listings that are broader than "Mental illness." If "Mental illness" has too few resources, you can try the subject headings in the BT list. In this example, you might look under the subjects of "Diseases," "Psychiatry," or "Psychology, Pathological."
- *RT:* This abbreviation means *related topic*. The subjects under the RT abbreviation are associated with the main subject but fall outside of the main term's hierarchy. If you are not finding what you want using "Mental illness," you might try "Mental health" in this example.
- *NT:* This abbreviation means *narrower topic*. The subjects listed under the NT notation are search terms that can be used that are more specific. If you find too many resources under the main subject of "Mental illness," you might narrow your search by using one of the subjects under the NT notation.
- *SA:* This abbreviation (not seen in the Figure 3-2 example) stands for *see also*. Subjects under the SA notation cover similar subjects.
- *USE:* This notation gives information about the correct subject heading in the *LCSH* listing. For example, if you see, under the subject "Mental Illness," that you might want to look up "surgery," the *USE* notation tells you that Psychosurgery is the appropriate heading for subjects about surgery and mental illness. Understanding this notation could save a significant amount of time by pointing you in precisely the right direction.
- *Hyphens:* All of the subject headings noted with a hyphen are subdivisions of the major listing to help you focus on the exact area of mental illness you want to explore.

3

Mental illness (*May Subd Geog*)

Here are entered popular works and works on social aspects of mental disorders. Works on the legal aspects of mental illness are under Insanity. Works on clinical aspects of mental disorders, including therapy, are entered under Psychiatry.

UF Diseases, Mental
Madness
Mental disorders
Mental diseases
BT Diseases
Psychiatry
Psychology, Pathological
RT Mental health
NT Dual diagnosis
Genius and mental illness
Insanity
Neurobehavioral disorders
— Alternative treatment
— Diagnosis
BT Psychodiagnostics
NT Psychiatric disability evaluation
— Epidemiology
USE Psychiatric epidemiology
— Prevention
— Surgery
USE Psychosurgery
— Treatment (May Subd Geog)
— Evaluation
NT Psychiatric rating scales

Figure 3-2 ***LCSH* Subject Entry.** An *LCSH* subject entry helps a researcher to narrow down a larger topic to specifically locate a library resource by how it is classified.

SELF-ASSESSMENT QUESTION

- What are some synonyms for the topic "Mental Illness" that you could use as an alternative search term?

SELF-ASSESSMENT QUESTION

- What key terms or term combinations could you use for a topic that you might be asked to research in your job or a course? Write down at least 10 key terms or term combinations that you could use to conduct a keyword search.

KEYWORD SEARCH

If you do not know an author or title, you can conduct a keyword search. The difference between a keyword and a subject is that the subject is limited to the specific Library of Congress subject heading assigned to the item, whereas a keyword is any word or word combination in the record.

A keyword search looks for specific keywords in all fields in a record and is used when you would like to look for a word or a combination of words simultaneously. In an OPAC, the keyword could be in the title, the author's name, the subject, or other places in the record. On the Internet, a keyword search brings up results that have that word or word combination anywhere in the document.

BOOLEAN OPERATORS

Boolean operators include the words "and," "or," and "not." These terms can be used in combination with keywords to broaden or narrow the search results by specifying exactly how you want the search to be conducted. Boolean operators can be used with most search engines, databases, and OPACs. A clear understanding of how these simple operators work can save a lot of time in using electronic searching tools.

Boolean operators work like a Venn diagram with words. A Venn diagram uses circles that stand alone or overlap to show logical relationships between concepts or ideas. Suppose you want to conduct a search using the search terms "film" and "theater." Each Boolean operator will narrow or broaden your search using keywords.

Figure 3-3 shows the use of the Boolean operator "AND." The operator "AND" is used to search for information on both film *and* theater. The results using these two keywords and the operator "AND" will bring up information that includes both film and theater. The correct notation you would use as your search terms would be *film AND theater*. The results would fall into the middle, shaded area created by the overlapping of the film and theater circles. There would be no results for only film and no results for only theater. This operator narrows the search by finding results that include both film and theater.

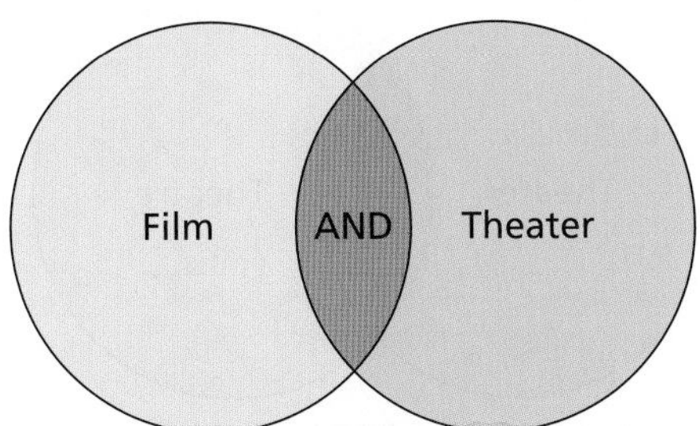

Figure 3-3 Boolean Searching Using "AND". Using the Boolean operator "and" gives the results that include both search terms.

3

Figure 3-4 shows the use of the Boolean operator "NOT." The "NOT" operator is used when you want to bring up information with one of the keywords, but you do not want information that includes the other keyword. In this example, searching for *film NOT theater* results in information about film only and does not bring up information about theater. Any results about film but also including the term "theater" will be omitted. This narrows the search significantly, saving time that might be wasted in sorting through information on film that also includes theater.

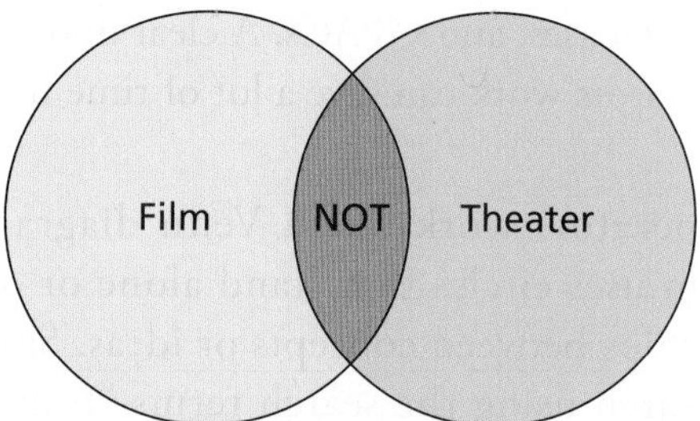

Figure 3-4 Boolean Searching Using "NOT". Using the Boolean operator "not" gives the results that include one search term but not the other.

Figure 3-5 shows the Boolean operator "OR", which can be used to broaden a search. For example, "theater" (T-H-E-A-T-E-R) has the accepted alternate spelling of "theatre" (T-H-E-A-T-R-E). If you want to make sure that the search returns information using both spellings, you would use the Boolean operator "OR", as in *theater OR theatre*. This will return information that includes both spellings of the word.

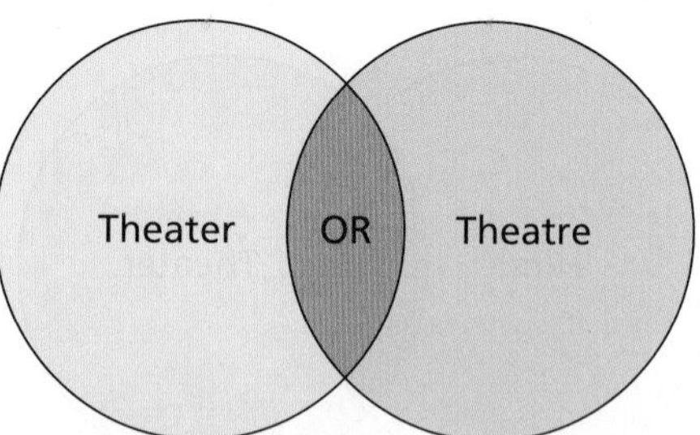

Figure 3-5 Boolean Searching Using "OR". Using the Boolean operator "or" gives results that include one search term or the other search term.

Combining Boolean operators can be useful at times. For example, if you want to search for information about film and either spelling of theater, you could use the "AND" operator combined with the "OR" operator, as in *film AND (theater OR theatre)*, as illustrated in Figure 3-6.

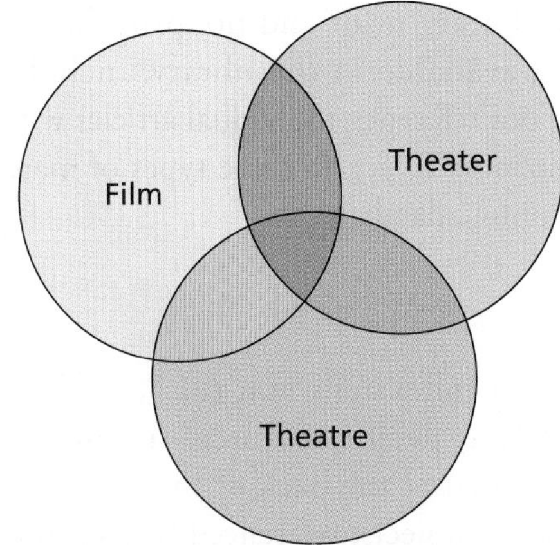

Figure 3-6 Boolean Searching Using "AND" and "OR". Using the Boolean operator "or" in combination with "and" expands your search.

There may be times in which you would like to find variants of a word. This can be accomplished by using a question mark (?) as a wildcard. For example, you would like to lookup variations of the word film, such as filmmaker. When you complete the search, you would enter the following: *film?*

It is also possible to complete more complex searches by using parentheses and multiple Boolean operators. Suppose you would like to lookup the theater production of *Chicago*, but not the film version. When completing the search, the following phrase should be used: *Chicago AND (theater NOT film).*

Implied Boolean operators include 1 in front of a word to retrieve results when the word is included and a 2 in front of the word to retrieve results where the word is excluded—similar to AND and NOT operators. Quotation marks around phrases sometimes are used to retrieve results when the specific phrase is included.

Boolean operators can be used with search engines to focus an online search. Most search engines also have an "Advanced Search" link, which is a useful and intuitive tool for focusing or narrowing your searches as well. The advanced search feature is convenient because

SELF-ASSESSMENT QUESTIONS

Go back to your own workplace research example.

- Using the keywords you listed and other appropriate terms, how could you narrow or broaden your search using only one operator?
- How can you combine your search terms using the Boolean technique to broaden your search? To narrow your search?

it allows you to accomplish the same goal as Boolean operators. For instance, in Google, there is an "all these words" field that allows you to enter what you're looking for without adding the Boolean term.

INDEXES

OPACs reference library print and nonprint holdings, that is the various resources available in the library, including periodicals; however, they do not reference individual articles within newspapers, journals, or magazines. To access these types of materials, you must have an index or online database.

Book Indexes

Like the OPAC, an index tells you the "address" or location of information within a specific resource. In nonfiction books, the index is usually located at the back of the book. A book's index is an alphabetical list of subjects, referenced by page numbers, showing where you can find that subject mentioned within the text. In a multivolume reference set, each volume may have its own index. Often, the index is a stand-alone index volume. Each subject in the alphabetical list in the index references the volume number and page number where the subject is mentioned in the resource.

For example, in a multivolume resource where the volumes are referenced by a separate index and volumes are separated alphabetically, "Abraham Lincoln" would be referenced as follows: Lincoln, Abraham L:259. The L is the volume letter, and 259 is the page number where the article about Abraham Lincoln begins.

Some indexes use only numbers. For example, in a multivolume reference set where the volume is referenced by volume numbers, information on Abraham Lincoln would be referenced as follows: Lincoln, Abraham 10/259. The number on the left is the volume number. The number on the right is the page number where the article begins.

In many cases, topics are discussed in multiple places. Additional references would be listed after the main subject listing, indented, such as:

Lincoln, Abraham L:259

Booth, John Wilkes B:300

Gettysburg Address G:128

Grant, Ulysses S. G:238

Periodical Indexes

A periodical index is a cumulative list of articles from a set of periodicals arranged in alphabetical order by author, title, or subject, and typically within a specified date range. The entries or citations provide all the information needed to find a specific article.

An important difference between a library's catalog or OPAC and a periodical index is that a periodical index is published by commercial entities and indexes a preestablished set of periodicals, whether or not the library it is in subscribes to all of the periodicals referenced in the index. Once you find an article you want to read in a periodical index, you have to check the OPAC of the library you are in to see if the library actually subscribes to that periodical. If so, you can go to the periodical area of the library, locate the periodical and specific volume, and read the article.

Typically, periodicals cannot be checked out of the library; however, you can make a photocopy of the article—if you adhere to copyright restrictions. In larger libraries, periodicals often are separated by current (periodicals recently received) and bound (periodicals bound together by volume or by time period). Older periodicals may even be in a different place entirely in the library, such as in the basement, as they are not used often and can take up a lot of space.

PUT IT TO USE Carefully read the signs posted in your library to see where the periodicals are located and how they are organized.

If the library does not subscribe to the periodical you want, you have the following three options:

1. Find a library that does subscribe to the periodical, and go there to read or copy the article.

2. Request that a copy of the article be sent to the home library through the library's interlibrary loan system. This usually involves a fee of a few dollars per page for copying, and often takes a few days to receive.
3. Access the article electronically using a full-text resource available either through the library or on the Internet. To find the article electronically, use an electronic version of the periodical index. Clicking on the title of the article typically brings up the full text, if it is available. Many online resources provide full-text articles either without charge or for a single-use or subscription fee. If the full-text version is not available, in many cases the abstract, or short summary, of the article can be read.

Thousands of periodical indexes cover more than 150,000 individual periodicals. Before you can begin searching for an article, you must find the appropriate index in which to search. General periodical indexes cover a broad range of topics in scholarly journals, popular magazines, and newspapers. Subject-specific periodical indexes cover articles in selected scholarly journals related to a broad topic or subject area.

As examples, the *Business Periodicals Index* references articles in the business arena and the *Index to Legal Periodicals* references legal-related articles. To find the most appropriate periodical index for your area of research, consult with your librarian. Figure 3-7 shows an example of a citation and the information you need to find the article in the actual periodical.

Critical Thinking Questions

Select a topic that you might want to research for one of your classes or for your career. Answer the following questions:

- In what subject area does my topic belong? (e.g., art, education, business, science)
- Do I need articles from professional journals or from popular magazines?
- Should I include both primary and secondary resources? Which would be best for my topic?
- Will my topic be covered in a general index, or should I look in subject-specific indexes?
- What indexes cover my subject or topic, and are they available at my library? In print? Electronically?
- How current does my information have to be?
- What indexes cover the necessary time periods?

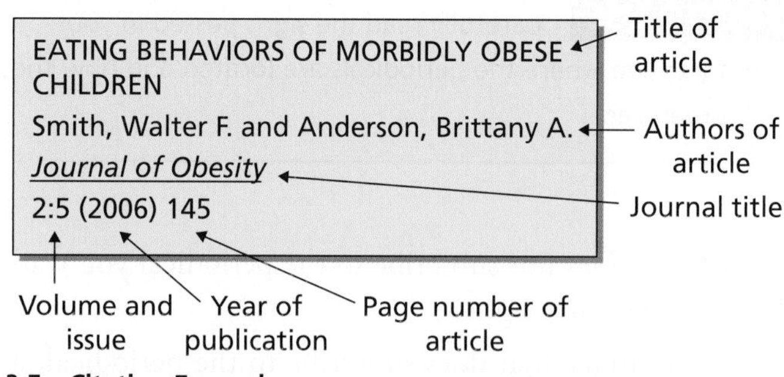

Figure 3-7 Citation Example.

success steps: using a periodical index

- Develop a list of keywords and subject headings for your topic.
- Determine the specific periodical index to use.
- Use the search word list and periodical index to find the exact citation for the article you want to read.
- Read the introductory material in a printed periodical index to see exactly how to use the periodical.
- Use the search tool in an electronic index and Boolean operators to narrow or broaden your search as needed.
- Go to the location in the library for the periodicals, and use the title of the periodical, the volume and page numbers listed in the citation, and the actual title of the article to find the article you want to read.
- Make a copy of the article, if needed.

If your library does not subscribe to the periodical you need, use the interlibrary loan system to have a copy of the article sent to your library.

DATABASES

A database is a collection of digitized information organized for simplified, fast searching and retrieval. A database may contain just a citation; a citation and abstract; or a citation, abstract, and full-text article. Like an OPAC, databases can be searched by subject, author, title, and keyword. Boolean operators typically can be utilized with databases, too, to broaden or narrow a search. When you are searching in a database, you can limit your search in numerous ways, including searching by the type of publication, by the date of the publication, by the publication itself, and so forth. You can print portions of a database, save the database to be accessed later, or email the database.

COLLECTING INFORMATION

Once you have developed your search statement and research questions, determined where to find the information, and accessed

3

the information, the next step is to collect the information from the information source. You can use several methods to collect your information.

SCANNING AND SKIMMING

Scanning and skimming are techniques for researchers who are exploring or seeking specific information. Scanning usually comes first and involves moving through material quickly to see if it contains what you need. If the scanning provides sufficient reason to do so, the researcher can go back and skim the information further. Use both scanning and skimming when you want to determine if an article is relevant to your research. Both scanning and skimming are good techniques when you have a lot of material to cover in a short time or if you have a lot of information to consolidate into a manageable amount.

Scanning is used to search for headings, keywords, ideas, or a specific piece of information. This technique is used when you know exactly what you are looking for and are concentrating on finding specific information. For example, when you are looking for a number or a name in a telephone book, you are scanning.

Skimming typically follows scanning but is equally important. Skimming is used to quickly determine the main idea in text by reading subheadings and the first sentences of sections and

success steps: skimming through a document

- Read the first and last paragraphs of the text.
- Read the titles, headings, and subheadings within the text.
- Read the first sentence of each paragraph.
- Look for names, dates, and places.
- Review nonfiction elements such as graphs, tables, charts, diagrams, and captions.
- Look for other organizational clues such as italicized words, bold print, and bulleted lists.
- Read any questions that may appear at the end of a text.

SELF-ASSESSMENT QUESTIONS

Select a chapter of a textbook that you are required to read for class in the next day or so. Scan the chapter, then skim the chapter. Then read the chapter fully.

- How much information do you think you got out of the chapter before you read it fully?
- Do you think that the scanning and skimming helped you in comprehending the information?

paragraphs. It allows the researcher to cover a great deal of information quickly and efficiently. It also gives the researcher an opportunity to determine whether more in-depth reading is necessary.

ONLINE HIGHLIGHTING

Highlighting is a technique that researchers use to mark important words, phrases, or passages of text for future use. Highlighting also can be used to discriminate between important information and interesting information. *Important information* is that which answers initial research questions or solves initial problems. *Interesting information* is that which the author uses to clarify the main points. As a researcher, you must be able to differentiate the two types of information and not be distracted by extraneous text. Excessive highlighting minimizes its effectiveness by obscuring the main ideas, so you should highlight only major concepts and key phrases.

If you conduct much of your research digitally, using online highlighting can be a very effective and time-saving tool. In addition to the ability to highlight text and images, some tools offer bookmarking and sticky note capabilities. One popular highlighting tool is Diigo (www.diigo.com).

KEEPING AND ORGANIZING INFORMATION ON THE COMPUTER

With all of the information that you are gathering for your research projects, it is important that you keep your files organized into some logical pattern on your computer or tablet so that you do not waste time searching for items.

One very handy tool that can help you make and keep sense of all of your information is an open-source bibliographic management tool called Zotero (www.zotero.org). Zotero allows users to collect, organize, cite, and share all of their research sources. You can collect PDFs, images, audio and video files, and parts of webpages, to name a few. It also automatically indexes the full-text content of what you have captured so you can find the files you are looking for quickly and easily.

Zotero allows you to create bibliographies and citations, and you can choose which publication format (such as Modern Language Association [MLA] or American Psychological Association [APA] to use. It can be downloaded for free, and it is compatible with Mac, Windows, and Linux.

CHAPTER SUMMARY

This chapter addressed several key issues as they pertain to finding and accessing information. You learned that in order to find information, you must first understand how libraries are organized, how the materials in libraries and on the Internet are cataloged and referenced, and how to access and efficiently use these reference tools.

This chapter also focused on the importance of understanding basic search techniques for finding information in libraries. Finally, you learned several effective techniques for collecting information from the information source.

POINTS TO KEEP IN MIND

In this chapter, several main points were discussed in detail:

- It is important to use librarian expertise when conducting research.
- There are many types of electronic resources that can be used to find information.
- Most library resources include four pieces of information: author, title, subject, and keyword. Each can be used to search for information.
- Boolean operators are a type of search method that include the words "and," "or," and "not." The use of these words can broaden or narrow a search.
- Types of library indexes include book indexes and periodical indexes.
- A database is a collection of digitized information organized for simplified, fast searching and retrieval.
- Three techniques for collecting information include scanning and skimming, online highlighting, and organizing information on the computer.

apply it

Activity #1 Reviewing and Revising the Search Process

Select or create a research project. Use the Research Skills Worksheet as a road map for research or problem solving. Write your response in the spaces provided. Then answer the following questions:

1. How did following this process help you find and access the information you needed?
2. As a result, do you think you were more efficient in your research?
3. What are the most difficult steps in this process? Why?

Research Skills Worksheet

Research Process	Task	Your Response
What is the problem or question to be addressed?	Write out clearly the specific assignment.	
What is the topic to be researched?	Write down your specific search statement.	
What questions have to be answered?	Write four research questions to accompany search statement.	
What key concepts have to be addressed?	Identify and write down two or three key concepts.	
What synonyms can be used for key concepts?	Write four to eight synonyms for key concepts.	
What perspective should be used to address the questions?	Determine the point of view—subjective, objective, multiple perspectives.	
How current does your information have to be?	Look at the questions and decide the importance of currency of the resource.	
What resources should be utilized?	List four to six specific resources to be used.	
Where are these resources located and accessed?	Write down call numbers for print resources, and access procedures for electronic resources.	
What means of information collection will be used?	Determine note-taking style, and record information.	
What information is needed to cite these sources?	Record the needed information for each source.	

Activity #2 Searching Practice: Part 1

Use the topic "computer literacy in the classroom" and a search engine on the Internet to practice searching for appropriate information.

continued

continued

1. What keywords should you use for this topic?
2. What are some synonyms for the keywords?

Type the words or phrases, and examine your results.

3. What words or phrases might you not want to include in your keywords?
4. How can you combine your search terms using Boolean operators to narrow or broaden your results?

Activity #3 Searching Practice: Part 2

Using the OPAC, find one *book* on a topic related to this class.

Title: ______________________________

Author: ______________ Call Number: ______________

Will this be a good source for the topic? Why or why not?

Find one article from a scholarly journal on the topic, using a periodical index.

Article Title: ______________________________

Author: ______________ Publication Date: ______________

Periodical Title: ______________________________

Periodical Index Utilized: ______________________________

Will this be a good source for the topic? Why or why not?

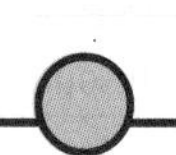

SUGGESTED ITEMS FOR LEARNING PORTFOLIO

Refer to the "How to Use This Book" section at the beginning of this textbook for more information on learning portfolios.

- Completed Research Skills Worksheet

REFERENCES

Cann, A., Dimitriou, K., and Hooley, T. (2011). *Social Media: A Guide for Researchers*. Retrieved February 29, 2016, from http://www.rin.ac.uk/system/files/attachments/social_media_guide_for_screen_0.pdf

Dictionary.com. (2016). *"Media Center."* Retrieved February 29, 2016, from http://dictionary.reference.com/browse/media-center?s=t

Library of Congress. (n.d. [a]). *About the Library*. Retrieved July 2, 2013, from http://www.loc.gov/about/

Library of Congress. (n.d. [b]). *Mobile Apps from the Library of Congress*. Retrieved January 25, 2016, from https://www.loc.gov/apps/

Laverty, S. (2016). *Advantages, Disadvantages and Risks of Deep Web Search Engines*. Retrieved February 1, 2016, from http://smallbusiness.chron.com/advantages-disadvantages-risks-deep-search-engines-74087.html

Regan, K. (2015). *10 Amazing Social Media Growth States from 2015*. Retrieved February 1, 2016, from http://www.socialmediatoday.com/social-networks/kadie-regan/2015-08-10/10-amazing-social-media-growth-stats-2015

Wikipedia.com. (2016). *Wikipedia: Ten Things You May Not Know about Wikipedia*. Retrieved February 1, 2016, from https://en.wikipedia.org/wiki/Wikipedia:Ten_things_you_may_not_know_about_Wikipedia

Emma Innocenti/Taxi/Getty Images

4

Evaluating Information

LEARNING OBJECTIVES

By the end of this chapter, you will be able to:

- Use a set of criteria to evaluate information and information sources.
- Identify specific criteria that should be used to evaluate webpages for credibility and appropriateness.

4

BE IN THE KNOW

Evaluate This!

Did you know that you can have a professional career as an evaluator? According to the American Evaluation Association (www.eval.org), an evaluator is someone who assesses the strengths and weaknesses of programs, personnel, policies, products, or organizations to improve their efficiency (American Evaluation Association, n.d.). Their website lists evaluation/evaluator/research job openings on its career page.

The following is a sampling of job titles associated with evaluation:

- Monitoring and Evaluation Consultant
- Manager, Research, and Evaluation
- Science, Technology, Engineering, and Math (STEM) Education and Evaluation Manager
- Senior Evaluation
- Evaluation Assistant
- Public Health Evaluator
- Senior Evaluation Officer
- Online Course Development Evaluator
- Director of Research and Evaluation
- Evaluation Analyst

Learning to properly evaluate information is one component of becoming information-literate. And who knows, it may end up becoming your career!

SOLVING INFORMATION PROBLEMS: EVALUATE THE INFORMATION

Information-literate individuals critically analyze information and its sources to ensure that it is useful. Critical analysis is applying rational and logical thought while deconstructing information to assess its value. When this process is not completed, it increases the risk of using inaccurate and inappropriate information, making poor decisions based on poor information, and losing time. Critical analysis applies to print materials and resources, multimedia resources, and content on the Internet. This chapter suggests several criteria you can use to analyze information and information sources as the next step in the research process. We will look first at criteria that can be applied to all

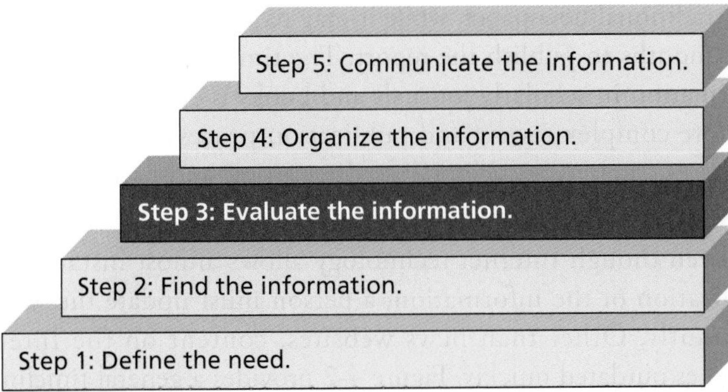

Figure 4-1 Research Process Step 3: Evaluate the Information. The third step of any research project should be to critically evaluate the information found.

4

information and then discuss tips that apply specifically to critiquing information found on the Internet. After you read this chapter, you should be able to apply critical analysis in asking questions about information sources, as well as provide criteria for evaluating those sources. This follows Step 3 of conducting effective research, as shown in Figure 4-1.

EVALUATING THE RESOURCE

Evaluating information is based in large part on common sense. Still, to understand the relevant criteria, it helps to understand how information is published and communicated.

PUBLICATION TIMELINE

The timeline for publishing information influences the content and defines how the information can be used effectively. Thus, the publication timeline becomes one of several criteria for evaluation. When an event occurs, radio and news agencies such as CNN may be able, via satellite systems, to give live reports of the event. Although not in real-time, online newspapers are also able to develop content for public consumption quickly. Traditional newspapers and magazines, however, take much longer to report the facts of the same event. You may need to wait until the following day to read the facts in a traditional newspaper, while it may require a magazine weeks or even months to publish the report. The timeline for publication of information in scholarly journals and books is even longer, because of more complex review and publication processes. Large-volume resources, such as encyclopedias, directories, and handbooks, may not be published for many months, if not years.

Even though Internet technology allows almost instantaneous publication of the information, a person must update the website constantly. Other than news websites, content on the Internet becomes outdated quickly. Figure 4-2 provides a general timeline of currency of the information.

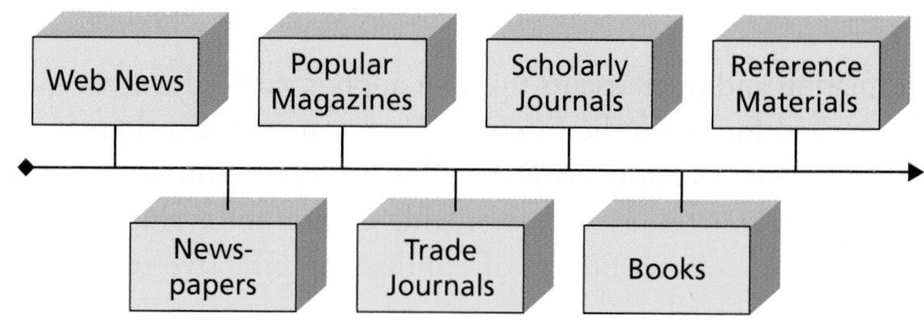

Figure 4-2 Publication Timeline.

Different kinds of information are needed for different purposes. Following are examples of the best formats for various types of information, based on flow and timing:

- *History.* History is an example of a topic that does not necessarily require up-to-the-minute information. For some projects, however, understanding historical facts is necessary. For example, if you are writing a report about an event in history, understanding the context in which that event occurred might be pivotal to the effectiveness of your finished project. You might want to know about the geographical area, the society and its culture, the political environment, the time period, and the area's demographics. Because this information does not change from the past, a book or an encyclopedia might be an excellent resource. Historical sites on the Internet would provide the same type of data. Conversely, if you are seeking a contemporary perspective on a historical event, a more recent information source would be more appropriate.

- *Technology*. Technology provides an example opposite from that of history. Because changes in technology occur rapidly, the material a book contains about a given technology is likely to be outdated by the time it is published. Take the example of a book describing a mobile app. A better app or an updated version of the software is likely to be available by the time the book is published. Better resources for this type of information would be through the website of the company that publishes the app, as well as reputable technology review sites, such as PC Magazine (PCMag.com) and Cnet.com.
- *Behind-the-scenes information*. In some cases, an understanding of what occurred just before an event is important. This kind of information may be in the form of personal correspondence (e.g., memos, emails, letters, electronic mailing lists), various types of documentation (e.g., diaries, journals, logs, personal notes, lab notes of an experiment), and other media (e.g., newsletters, conference programs). While some behind-the-scenes information is readily available (e.g., blog), many of the other aforementioned sources are not always easy to find or access. This may require a researcher to contact individuals, such as historians, museum curators, reference librarians, and archives and records administrators directly as part of his or her information gathering process. Despite the potential inconvenience involved in acquiring this type of information, it can often play an important role in explaining why an event occurred or documenting the chronology of events.
- *Immediate information (minutes)*. Live news sources, such as those found on the Internet, provide immediate information. In many cases, the facts of the event (who, what, where, when, how) are provided, but the background or "why" of the event may not be known yet. This kind of information has to be critiqued carefully, as live reporting may be inaccurate when there is little time to check the facts. The prevalence of social media has also increased the need for careful examination of information. For example, tweets made on Twitter and posts via Facebook provide almost instantaneous reporting of an incident, but that speed can also increase the ease in which misinformation is spread.

- *Current information (days)*. Current information includes material that is reported a few hours to a few days after an event. TV and radio reporting, newspaper reporting, and online reporting all provide this type of information. There may have been time to research the background of the event and to check the facts. The content may also include analysis, statistics, interviews, historical context, and other relevant information.
- *Older information (weeks)*. Magazines provide information several days to weeks after an event. Because these sources take longer to publish the content, they allow sufficient time to check facts, research the background and historical context, find supporting data, conduct interviews, and enhance the information. Often these sources report for a specific purpose, so the content must be reviewed for bias or a specific slant. The information is less current than live or next-day reports, and although there is time to check facts, accuracy is not guaranteed.
- *Older information (months to years)*. Information that is several months, or even years, old is published in scholarly journals, conference papers, research reports, and books. These information sources require time to conduct detailed studies or analyses of data or events, review by peers or editors, and physical publication of the resources. Journals and conference papers that are found online adhere to the same process, so the time requirement is similar. An advantage is that these resources can provide more detailed, thorough, and accurate information.
- *Older information (years)*. Information that is several years old typically is published in book form. Researching and writing a book may take months to years, followed by additional time for review, editing, and production. This type of resource can provide accurate and detailed content with supporting background, analysis, and commentary. Typically, books provide much more information than the forms previously described. They can support one perspective or provide numerous viewpoints. Currency of the information is sacrificed for volume and depth.

- *Reference resources.* Publications such as encyclopedias, handbooks, and statistical compilations all provide factual and typically unbiased information. These sources sacrifice currency for detail and accuracy. They require time to check the facts and ensure accuracy, compile the information, and publish the resource. Sometimes these kinds of resources can be found on the Internet, but, like online journals, they require time for gathering and organizing the material, and additional time to input the data into a database.

SELF-ASSESSMENT QUESTIONS

- Think about your academic or workplace information needs. When might you need each of the aforementioned types of information?
- What is an example of a resource in your field of study for each type of information?

TYPES OF RESOURCES

Journals and magazines are common sources of information. The three basic types of journals and magazines are: (1) scholarly journals, (2) trade publications, and (3) popular magazines. Each of these types has a different purpose and target audience. Collectively, they hold a wealth of useful information, but it is important to recognize the differences between and among them to critically evaluate the appropriateness of their content.

Scholarly Journals

Scholarly journals are written by authorities in a topic area or field of study and include research reports and other academic or factual information. The main purpose of a scholarly journal is to report original, current research data to individuals in the scholarly and professional arenas. Scholarly research means that scientists and researchers have conducted highly structured studies using accepted methods and have made educated, justifiable conclusions about the results. These scientists and researchers typically work for educational institutions, such as colleges and universities, or for private research organizations, such as research labs, think tanks, hospitals, and non-profit groups. In their articles, they use the language and technical terminology associated with the specific field. They also employ a structured format and follow accepted guidelines for studying a specific topic. The research results in qualitative data, which describe the characteristics or observations of something, or quantitative data, which measure something.

In many cases, the articles are sent out to reviewers who are specialists in the field. They analyze the information, methods, results, and conclusions that the authors have drawn. The reviewers make recommendations to the publisher that the manuscript be accepted, revised in some way, or rejected because of poor study design or invalid conclusions. The review provides expert appraisal, and although the review does not guarantee accuracy, it does provide a check on the content, adding to the information's credibility. Poor research or inaccurate content has less chance of being accepted for publication in a scholarly journal than in other, less-structured types of journals or magazines. A journal that uses this review system is called a refereed or peer-reviewed journal. Journals that employ this level of rigor are typically highly credible.

Critical Thinking Questions

- What are five refereed journals that apply to your field of study? How do you know they are refereed? (Consider using Google or another online search engine, or talk to your reference librarian, to find at least five examples that might be useful in your research activities. Many journals have websites describing their publications.)
- What are five journals that are not refereed? How do you know they do not use a peer review process?

Examples of the many hundreds of scholarly journals are as follows:

- *Journal of the American Medical Association* (commonly called *JAMA*)
- *Journal of Geology*
- *Reviews of Modern Physics*
- *Journal of Infectious Disease*
- *Journal of Computer Information Systems*
- *Journal of International Business Studies*
- *Journal of Interior Design*
- *The American Professional Constructor*

Authors whose articles are published in scholarly journals are required to follow a structured format for organizing and publishing an article. Each scholarly journal has a set of guidelines informing authors how their manuscript should be submitted. These guidelines can be found in the journal itself or obtained from the publisher or the journal's website. Editors of the scholarly journal assess the quality and appropriateness of each article against these guidelines to determine appropriateness for publication.

To illustrate how reviews and manuscript guidelines are used, consider the following examples: The *Journal of Nutrition Education and Behavior* sends three reviewers a manuscript addressing the topic of food behavior. These reviewers might be university professors who teach in nutrition programs and who have completed research and published their own articles on a nutrition behavior topic. Other appropriate reviewers could be nutritionists who are familiar with food behaviors and psychologists who specialize in this area.

Regardless of their professional position, all reviewers are selected based on their expertise in nutrition behavior theories and the kinds of studies they have completed in the past. The reviewers also have access to the journal's guidelines, so they are knowledgeable about how the manuscript should be organized. The reviewers know how sound behavior studies should be organized and how to objectively assess the assumptions and conclusions from the data. They have a high level of education and have had substantial training in the topic area and in research design.

As reviewers of articles, their goal is to critically and objectively evaluate the assumptions, methods, and conclusions to ensure that only sound information is published. The reviewers often make suggestions to the authors, who then have the opportunity to implement the suggestions and thereby improve the quality of the article before publication.

This peer review process maintains the credibility of scientific investigation and reporting. A goal of scientific researchers is to publish articles about their research. Publishing an article lets the scientific community know what they are doing. The scientific community then reports the results of the study to the general population. Standards for activities such as manufacturing and legislation are based on current published and accepted research. Without publication, researchers' efforts go unrecognized and the information does not get implemented into daily life. If the researchers do not conduct sound research and use the data appropriately, their studies do not get published. The entire system provides an important check and balance for all of us.

A close look at the organization of a scholarly journal article and the purpose of each part of the article will help you develop your ability to gain useful information. A review of the *Guidelines for Authors* available for almost every scholarly journal will show that articles in these journals are required to be structured in a similar fashion. Most accounts of research are presented in a format similar to what is described next.

Abstract. An abstract is a brief synopsis of the article. In business proposals and other documents, the abstract is commonly called the executive summary. An abstract typically is limited to a specified length (e.g., 500 words) and must include the basic components or facts of the article. It provides the context and reasons for doing the study or writing the article. A good abstract explains briefly how the study was accomplished, identifies the major results, and states the conclusion. It also may state briefly why the study is important. Reading the abstract of a scholarly journal article before delving into the entire article can save a significant amount of time by revealing whether the information is appropriate for your purpose. If you determine that the article is appropriate, you then can read the article in its entirety for more details.

Keywords. Many scholarly journals include a list of words that helps to identify the main concepts in the article. These keywords show how the article has been categorized in various search engines and library indexes. In the example of the behavior change article, keywords might include: *behavior change theory*, *nutrition behavior*, *eating behavior*, *weight loss*, and *obesity*. These keywords can be used to search for articles on similar topics in journal indexes and search engines.

Introduction. Most journal articles begin with an introduction explaining why the authors have conducted the study or written the article and why the information is important. For example, in our nutrition behavior article, the author may start with a brief discussion of obesity as a significant problem in the United States, partially caused by poor nutrition. Most introductions end in some kind of purpose statement or thesis statement for the article. These statements explicitly state the intent of the study or article. In formal scientific studies, the purpose statement is replaced by a hypothesis, in which the authors make a statement that they will attempt to support with the results of their specific study.

Literature review. The literature review comes after the introduction and provides a brief overview of the relevant studies or articles that support or provide background information on the current study. The purpose of the literature review is to provide a solid foundation for the topic, using published information. One of the goals of scientific research is to add to the scientific body of knowledge in the field. Demonstrating the relationship of the current study to existing research clarifies that correlation and summarizes the scientific body of knowledge that relates specifically to the topic of the current study. The author must objectively review highlights, relevant findings, issues, controversies, successes, or failures of previous research.

For example, in the behavior change article, a thorough and informative literature review would highlight several behavior change theories or studies, including those that did not succeed. The author would be careful not to skew the perception to support the purpose of the study. Excellent literature reviews start out with a broad scope, and then narrow the focus specifically to the need for the current study or article.

Some articles are written for the sole purpose of discussing previous literature. These are called review articles. In the nutrition behavior example, a review article might highlight the major nutrition behavior theories studied in the past. Review articles do not include a methods section or a results section as described next. The review article is an excellent starting place for researching a scientific topic.

Methods. After the context and need for the study have been discussed in the introduction and the highlights from relevant previous studies have been summarized, the author explains in detail how the current study was conducted. Sound research methods contribute to the validity and reliability of the study. In addition, if another researcher wants to re-create the study, he or she could follow the methods described in the article. The description of the methods also allows the article's reviewers to determine if the study was conducted in a logical manner and if sound research standards and procedures were followed. If a tool, such as a questionnaire, was used, it should be included as an exhibit at the end of the article. If it is not included, readers should be able to contact the authors to gain access to the tool that was used.

Results. This section logically follows the methods section. Here, the author presents the results of the study in an objective, logical manner. Visual representations of data, such as tables, charts, graphs, diagrams, or photographs, are used frequently to illustrate the information. These types of infographics can be created by hand, but more often are developed using computer software, such as Adobe Illustrator. Establishing a direct correlation between the methods section and the results is vital to the study's credibility. The charts or tables should be labeled clearly and organized so readers can easily understand what is being communicated without reading the text of the article. Including graphical representations whenever possible and appropriate can only add to the clarity of the information.

Discussion. The next section in the article consists of a discussion of the results. Here, the author explains the results, discusses any problems that arose during the study that might have influenced the results, presents any unexpected event or finding, and relates the results back to the original findings in the literature. In some cases, the findings are supported by the literature review. In other cases, the findings contradict previous findings. In the event of a discrepancy, the author typically provides an explanation of the contradiction to the best of his or her ability. In most cases, the author makes an educated assumption about the findings, regardless of whether the findings supported or contradicted previous research.

Conclusions. Finally, the conclusions section explains the major inferences that can be drawn logically from the study and outlines why the findings are important to the industry or the general population. Authors often make recommendations for future research, including other topics that can be studied formally to help answer the research question or expand on the findings. A conclusion must be supported directly by results of the study versus the author's opinion.

References. Authors of articles in scholarly journals are required to state in their articles exactly where they get any information or facts. The source of a fact is indicated in the text of the article where the fact occurs and is called a citation. The complete source for the citation is provided in the reference list at the end of the article. Each journal provides its own style guide, including, among other requirements, specifically how to cite sources. Information on style guides is presented in the Legal and Ethical Issues Related to Information chapter.

Citing references appropriately credits authors of original work and is essential to avoid plagiarism (stealing the work or ideas of others). Plagiarism is highly unethical, illegal, and can lead to being reprimanded, fired, or sued. Using information that has been verified by others is acceptable and necessary to substantiate new research, but the original author or source of the information must be given proper credit.

Trade Publications

Trade publications (sometimes called trade journals) can be excellent sources of information, but they must be viewed critically for accuracy, credibility, and appropriateness. Authors of trade publications typically are specialists or practitioners in a given field. They write their articles for others in the same industry who face the same issues and have the same informational needs. Most information in trade publications is practical in nature, reporting on issues such as procedures, materials, technology, equipment, events, and policies or processes.

Typically, trade publications have no formal review process other than the basic editorial review, which ensures that the article is well-written and does not contain grammatical and typographical errors. In these publications, authors use the technical language of the field because the article is written for other industry professionals. Information is presented in charts, graphs, diagrams, and photographs, as appropriate. Although the authors often mention where they acquired their information, some do not cite their resources formally, in which case it may be difficult to find the original or primary source.

It is important to note that the trade publication industry, as with the newspaper business, has been steadily increasing its online presence, with some companies choosing to no longer offer printed versions.

A few examples of the many hundreds of trade publications are as follows:

- *Advertising Marketing and Research Reports*
- *Industrial Equipment News*
- *Concrete Products*
- *Building Design and Construction*
- *Business Solutions*
- *Computer Graphics World*
- *Veterinary Practice News*
- *Hospitality Technology*

4

CRITICAL THINKING QUESTIONS

- What trade publications are available in your field? Are any of them only available online?
- How can you use the information from these types of publications appropriately?

Popular Magazines

Popular magazines are the least useful type of journal/magazine for credible research. The main purpose of the articles in popular magazines is entertainment, to get readers to purchase the magazine, or perhaps to sway the reader to a specific way of thinking or point of view. Authors of the articles in popular magazines are writers on staff with the magazine and are rarely specialists in the topic area. In addition, freelance writers, who typically are not specialists in any one area, sell their articles to the magazine for a fee. Freelance writers conduct research and interviews to find the information needed for a specific article. They are writers, not authorities, with a goal of entertaining or informing the general population, resulting in increased sales and profits for the publication.

The language of the article typically is not as technical, because the target audience is usually the general public. As is the situation with trade journals, popular magazines have no review process other than the editorial review to ensure that the articles are well-written and free of grammatical and typographical errors. Even though some authors mention their sources of information, they rarely cite these sources formally, as is required in a scholarly journal. Often, numerous photographs are used instead of the charts and graphs presenting quantitative data.

You should be cautious in using information from popular magazines. There is no guarantee that the content is accurate, unbiased, or appropriate, and it can be difficult to verify facts or find the original or primary source of information in the absence of formal resource citations. Still, popular magazines are useful in some areas of research and for some types of information. For example, an interior designer can use popular magazines to keep up with current and geographical trends in design, materials, and techniques. Popular magazines also commonly include interviews with leaders in the field, provide current news and discussion of issues, and follow market trends.

A few examples of the hundreds of popular magazines are as follows:

- *Men's Health*
- *Smithsonian*
- *National Geographic*
- *Entrepreneur Magazine*
- *Popular Science*

- *Wired*
- *PC Magazine*
- *Sports Illustrated*
- *Scientific American*
- *The New Yorker*

CRITICAL THINKING QUESTIONS

- What popular magazines publish information related to your field?
- How can you use the information from these popular magazines appropriately?

questions to ask about evaluating sources

- When did the actual event occur?
- How current is the information in your source?
- What kind of information is needed? What is the purpose of the information?
- How current should the information be?
- What is the best source of information based on the publication's timeframe?
- Do you have to find the original or primary sources of information?
- What is the purpose of the publication you are using for your research?
- Has the publication put its articles through a formal peer review?

EVALUATING AUTHORITY

After determining the kind of resource you want to use, the next step in evaluating your information is to determine the authority of its author. The intention of this process is to look critically at the author of the information, as well as the sponsor or owner of the specific resource, such as the publisher or owner of a website. This process has become particularly important when examining web-based resources due to the fact that the overall growth in online content has resulted in an increase in sources written by authors presenting misinformation and biases as facts and analysis. Your goal is to determine if those who write the information are qualified to do so and whether they provide credible information. Several elements should be evaluated when considering the author and the publisher of a book or article, or the sponsor or owner of a website.

AUTHOR

In many information sources, the author's name is displayed prominently—on the front and title page of a book, on the first page of journal articles, and as a byline of newspaper and magazine articles. Some sources, such as encyclopedias and reference materials, have a number of authors, as well as a group of contributors or an editorial board that oversees the information submitted.

Several clues will help you determine an author's authority, which will give you an idea about the credibility of the information:

4

- *Expertise.* Look for signs that the author is an expert in the topic area and brings knowledge to the material. Expertise can come from academic degrees, work experience, previous publications, and extensive research. Consider conducting an online search using the author's name to find any organizations with which the author is associated, other publications he or she has written, news stories about the author, or other references. For some fields, biographical references provide information about many experts in a variety of fields. For example:
    - *Contemporary Authors*, by Thomson-Gale Publishers, provides biographical and bibliographical information on fiction and nonfiction authors.
    - Marquis *Who's Who* publishes biographical references in many different professional fields and geographical areas.
- *Academic background and credentials.* Look for evidence that the author has a credible academic background and qualifications for writing on the topic. Self-proclaimed experts or those who are merely impassioned about a topic may not be qualified to write about it. In research, a credible author might have a Ph.D. (or at least a Master's degree) in a related field, signifying that he or she conducts research or teaches in the area. In medically related areas, the author might be an M.D. or other medical professional with a qualified background pertaining to the topic.

- *Work-related or other experience.* In the business world, clues to credibility might be evident in work experience rather than academic credentials. Many credible websites have "Biography" sections listing the author's work-related experience. The company or organization's website may also provide additional information about the author. If the author is a professor at a university, for example, you might find out past and current research topics, courses taught, and committees on which the author serves. You can also conduct an online search to see if the author's name is associated with a company or professional organization. In most search engines, putting the name in quotes facilitates the search. For example, try a Google search for "Bob Smith".
- *Licensure or certification.* In some areas, an author might have a license or certification in a specific area, such as an Microsoft Certified Solutions Expert (MCSE), which indicates that he or she has passed an examination in Microsoft operating systems. If you find a credential and want to see if it is valid, conduct a search using the credential's name or letters to find the sponsoring organization and the explanation of the specific credential. Most organizations state exactly what the certified individual must know to gain and maintain certification and also may provide a list of currently certified individuals in a directory. For some professions, such as those in healthcare or financial fields, professionals are often licensed or otherwise regulated by the state. Maintaining a state credential frequently requires meeting continuing education or other professional certification requirements. Searching a database of state-credentialed professionals in a specific field can provide information regarding an individual's credibility.
- *Affiliation.* Look for the author's affiliations, such as with academic institutions, professional organizations, government agencies, and other professional groups. Authors who are affiliated with recognized organizations tend to be more credible. In many fields of study, professionals are expected to maintain membership in professional organizations. Also, check the affiliation itself. For example, Texas International University and the American Heart Disease Association sound

credible, but they are not real, even though the names are similar to authentic and highly credible organizations. Research the organization if you are not familiar with it and its purpose.

- *Other publications*. In some cases it is useful to find out what other publications to which the author has contributed or produced. A simple search using the author's full name in quotes on google.com may turn up additional publications. Books typically have an "About the Author" page or information on the book jacket that provides a list of the author's previous publications. Reputable authors are also often cited by other scholars.
- *Contact information*. In many publications, information about the author is available so you can contact the author either directly or through the publisher of the resource. Look for telephone numbers, mailing addresses, and email addresses.
- *Social media*. Some authors may maintain a public Facebook page, Twitter profile, or personal website containing useful information. Many will also have a LinkedIn account that provides information about their backgrounds and accomplishments as well as recommendations and peer testimonials.

Critical Thinking Questions

- Think about your field of study. What credentials would you expect for authors of credible information? Where should you be able to find this type of information?
- What academic background, work experience, academic degree, license, or affiliations would you expect? Why?

PUT IT TO USE An email address with no other information is not sufficient for assessing an author's credibility. Anyone can easily create an email address. If this is the only resource available, consider emailing the author to see if you can obtain additional information.

PUBLISHER

Another significant component of authority is the publisher of the resource. The publisher is responsible for the actual publication or website in which the information is located. Resources can be published by a university press, a trade press, a governmental agency, a not-for-profit organization, a specialized press, or an individual. Academic print products often are published by university presses, which tend to be scholarly and highly reputable. These publishers put their materials through a formal and rigorous screening to ensure that they meet the standards and goals of the publishing organization. The content often undergoes a peer review, which gives it credibility. Trade presses publish trade journals and magazines, which tend to be less formal in their review of information and typically do not require a peer review of their content.

Information published by a government agency is generally credible. For example, the U.S. Government Printing Office (GPO) publishes numerous materials to keep Americans informed about the activities of the three branches of government. You can find information published by the GPO at its website (www.gpo.gov). Among the numerous materials published by the GPO are the Budget of the United States Government, congressional bills, economic indicators, and the United States Code. Just about anything you want to know about the government that is available to the public can be found here.

Another type of publisher is the subsidy publisher. Also known as a vanity press, these publishers charge authors a fee to publish their work. In contrast to a traditional publisher, which accepts the risk of publication and ensures high-quality materials by providing editorial services and marketing or distribution of the product, the role of the subsidy publisher usually is limited to actual production of a book. The editorial and marketing tasks are the author's responsibility. Products from joint venture publishers can be of excellent quality, and many well-received books have come from these publishers. As with any resource, however, you must assess the accuracy, quality, and credibility of the information.

Critical Thinking Questions

- Go to the U.S. GPO at www.gpo.gov. Think carefully about your area of study. What are 10 different information sources published by the GPO that you might find useful in your job or academic courses?
- Who are the best-known publishers of information in your area of study?

Self-Assessment Questions

- Why would someone want to publish his or her materials through a subsidy press?
- What advantages and disadvantages would this kind of publishing have?

Critical Thinking Questions

- Visit the website of a subsidy publisher. What guidelines are required for publishing something?
- What services does the publisher provide to the author?

SPONSOR OR OWNER

In addition to researching the author and publisher, you should investigate the sponsor or owner of the resource. This is especially important when assessing websites. A sponsor may be an organization or an individual. A large and reputable organization, such as the American Heart Association, tends to be more credible than an unknown individual. Also, determine if the sponsor advocates a specific viewpoint or philosophy. This information usually can be found in the "Home" or "About Us" portion of a website or on promotional print materials.

Critical Thinking Questions

- When researching information in your field, what kind of sponsor or owner would you expect to be credible? Why? Give some examples.
- When researching information in your field, what kind of sponsor or owner would you be highly suspicious of? Why? Give some examples.

4

When evaluating sponsors, look carefully at *why* they are presenting the information. This is important for print and digital resources alike. Does the sponsor have a mission associated with the content? For example, the mission statement of the American Heart Association is "to build healthier lives, free of cardiovascular diseases and stroke" (American Heart Association, n.d.). You would expect credible information on health, disease, and related material from this association. Because it is a not-for-profit agency, it does not have the ulterior motive of selling products or making money from sponsoring this information. In contrast, a manufacturer of a healthcare product is in the business of making money by selling that product. Therefore, information sponsored by this kind of organization should be examined thoroughly to determine the accuracy and credibility of the content.

PUT IT TO USE Just because an entity sells a product or makes money from the information does not mean that their claims are biased or inaccurate; it only means that you should check out the information carefully and keep in mind the purpose of the organization.

questions to ask about evaluating authority

- Who is the author?
- What are the author's academic credentials related to the topic?
- What is the author's experience related to the topic?
- What kind of credential(s) does the author have (such as a license or certificate)?
- What is the author's affiliation?
- What else has the author published?
- Is the author well known in the field?
- Is information provided so you can contact the author?
- Who is the publisher, and what kinds of materials are published?

- Who is the sponsor or owner (especially of websites), and is that sponsor stable?
- What is the sponsor's philosophy?
- Is the sponsor suitable to address this topic?
- Did the author prepare this information as a part of his or her professional duties or have some other relationship with the sponsor?

EVALUATING CURRENCY

4

Currency refers to the timeliness of the information. For a print product, currency is determined by date of publication. As you will recall, different types of publications require different timelines. To review—newspapers are published a few hours after the event. Books can take months or even years to be printed, so the date of publication must be viewed in light of the type of information resource. Although webpages can take much less time to publish, it is difficult sometimes to determine the currency of the information. Recall as well that an information-literate individual understands how current the information has to be for the specific purpose. For some needs, the information must be as up-to-date as possible. For other purposes, such as historical research, currency is not important.

Additional clues can be found within the information itself. Look carefully at the references the author uses. A journal article that has been published recently but uses references from 10 years ago is not likely to be as current as one that uses more recent references. In the scientific community, many changes and advancements can happen in a short time. Also, look for clearly dated information. For example, if the article refers to a statistic about computer use in public schools, check the date of the original source. If that statistic is from 1980, it is not relevant today. Some information that is older may be fine depending on its type. The important part is that you carefully evaluate the type of information you are using and make a judgment on its currency and relevance to your topic.

Critical Thinking Questions

- Think about a specific research project that you have to do in school or in your job. How current did this information have to be?
- For this project, what kinds of information sources would be best to use? Specifically, how would you determine the currency of the information?

questions to ask about evaluating currency

- How current does the information have to be?
- What is the date of publication of the resource?
- What is the edition of the resource?
- Can you determine the currency of the original source of the information by looking at the references?
- Is the sponsoring organization stable, meaning is it a viable organization that will probably be around for a while?

DATE AND EDITION OF A PUBLICATION

In a print product, look for the copyright date on the reverse side of the title page. Determine if the date is appropriate for the topic. Many information sources are revised periodically with minor changes for reprinting, or new editions are published with more significant changes. More than one edition indicates that the material has been updated to reflect new information and to correct mistakes. Multiple editions suggest a more reliable resource because the publisher chooses to continue to publish the book's subsequent versions.

EVALUATING THE CONTENT

After you have evaluated the resource itself, the authority of the author, and the currency, you will examine various aspects of the content itself. When looking critically at the content, you should appraise for whom the material was written, purpose and scope of the information, objectivity of the information, and its accuracy and verifiability. Examining these characteristics in-depth will illustrate their importance in the evaluation process.

INTENDED AUDIENCE

A first step is to determine the intended audience for whom the information was written. In general, it is written for specialists in the field, practitioners, a general audience or the general public, an educated audience, or some kind of specialized group. On the one hand, information that is highly technical is intended for clinicians, physicians, technicians, or practitioners. It may be too technical for laypersons or for an overview of a topic. On the other hand, information that is too general and is written for the general public may not be useful to a practitioner or researcher who requires detailed, technical materials. The intended audience of the information and the information source dictate the type, depth, and focus of the content. In general, you should ask if the content is sufficiently scholarly to meet your goal but not so technical that it is too difficult to understand.

Self-Assessment Questions

- Who are the various intended audiences for information in your field of study?
- For each audience, what is the level and focus of the writing and content?

PURPOSE AND SCOPE

The next step is to look at the information to try to understand its purpose. Why was the information written or produced in the first place? Was the goal to inform, entertain, trick, sell, persuade, or damage? Some sources are created to provide new information; other sources are created to update existing knowledge. In many cases, content is written so it provides only one side or view of an issue. Other resources provide a balanced treatment of all sides of an issue.

Self-Assessment Question

- Think about a topic that you might research in your field of study. For the topic you select, what information would be considered as background or an overview? What information would provide more focused details?

questions to ask about evaluating content

- Who is the intended audience?
- Is the tone and treatment of the information appropriate for the intended audience?
- Are the terms and concepts too technical to understand?
- Are the terms and concepts too simplified to be useful?
- Are the depth and detail sufficient for the needs of the audience?
- What is the purpose of the information?
- Do you detect ulterior motives, such as selling, persuading, damaging, and so forth?
- Is the information a primary source or a secondary source?
- What is the scope of the information?

Scope refers to how broad or narrow the topic is. An overview topic typically is broad in scope, with few details. A narrowly focused treatment of the topic gives details on a small portion of a larger topic. This is why you have to thoroughly understand your need for the information, and then decide how in-depth the information has to be. For scholarly journals, review articles give an overview of the major findings of a topic. Each article referenced in the overview article follows with details on a narrow subtopic. In many research projects, broadly scoped sources are sufficient for describing the context or background of a topic. Then, more narrowly focused sources are used to detail the main topic of the project.

OBJECTIVITY

When evaluating content, you will have to determine whether information is fact or opinion. Facts are things that can be proven to have happened or to exist. Opinions are statements or judgments or beliefs, which may or may not be true. Facts should be backed up by a credible source and should be verifiable. You could go to a primary source to find the same information. Keep in mind, though, that opinions can be written to look as if they are facts.

PUT IT TO USE You should look at the facts the author provides, as well as facts the author does not provide. For example, an author may provide accurate facts about the benefits of taking a specific medication for a disease but leave out the serious side effects of taking the medication. Another author might alert you to the possible side effects as well as the benefits.

Information is often presented from a specific point of view. In a neutral point of view, only the facts are presented, without bias. Bias means that the facts are presented with prejudice. A source should be critiqued to see if it has any prejudice or bias in the way it is presented. For example, if a health food store publishes a newsletter highlighting the benefits of taking the vitamins sold in the store but fails to discuss any research suggesting that taking the vitamins have no benefits or negative consequences, the newsletter has a biased point of view. Opinion pieces, commentaries, and book reviews are all written with a specific point of view.

Most news agencies are said to have one point of view or another (e.g., conservative or liberal). You will have to study the content to determine the point of view. An additional method is to visit the website of the *Pew Research Center* (www.pewresearch.org; 2016), a nonpartisan fact tank, to review the results of comprehensive surveys indicating which news agencies Americans feel are most trusted, as well as a recent ranking of agencies on a scale from liberal to conservative. Regardless of your approach, content should be evaluated based on whether the author conveys personal emotions or prejudices, makes unjustified claims or excessive claims of certainty, or distorts facts to support a point of view.

CRITICAL THINKING QUESTIONS

- In your area of study, how might information providers be biased? Give specific examples.
- What are controversial topics or issues in your field about which authors might show emotion or have extreme views?

4

PUT IT TO USE Biased information is not necessarily bad information, but it is essential to recognize bias and then seek out the opposite viewpoint so you will have a clear understanding of the entire issue or topic.

questions to ask about evaluating objectivity

- Is the information presented fairly and from a neutral point of view?
- Is there a specific motive for presenting the information?
- Are all sides of a story presented?
- Who is the author, and why is he or she presenting the information?
- What is the purpose of the information?
- Are facts and statements justified and backed up with sound research or primary sources?
- Is the author moderate or extreme in presenting the views?
- Is there a conflict of interest?
- If there is advertising, is it appropriate and separate from the objective information?

ACCURACY AND VERIFIABILITY

Along with objectivity, you will have to determine if the information is accurate and whether it can be verified with another credible resource. Accuracy covers a wide scope including:

- accurate facts
- accurate reference to other resources
- no typographical errors
- no grammatical or punctuation errors
- logical assumptions
- logical flow of information
- logical conclusions based on information
- accurate visual aids, such as charts, graphs, and diagrams
- appropriate coverage of material

PUT IT TO USE Look to see if the author can be contacted to verify facts or answer clarifying questions.

Verifiable means that the information is based on facts that can be authenticated by another credible source or several credible sources.

The best information cites the original or primary source. The sources have to be available for checking to verify that they exist and actually support the statements and facts in the content. On a webpage, check the links to see if they go to where they say they will go and if the linked source is also credible. For print references, consider checking the listed references to ensure that they support what has been stated. Also, compare the facts or statements made in one source with what is generally accepted.

For example, consumption of high-fat foods and lack of exercise are generally recognized as increasing the risk for heart disease. A resource that states otherwise goes against what is accepted to be true in the scientific community. Though new uses of technology and discoveries can result in changes to generally accepted ideas, these statements must be evaluated before accepting them.

PUT IT TO USE If an information resource does not enable you to readily check the references, be suspicious of the information.

OVERALL QUALITY

In addition to accuracy of the information, the overall quality has to be evaluated, assessing the structure of the document and how the content is arranged. High-quality information is arranged in a logical and consistent manner. It is broken down into logical sections or parts and is well laid out. Headings describe the content accurately. Visual aids, such as graphs, photos, charts, and tables, provide additional information and do not distract readers from the material. Visual aids are able to stand alone; you can understand the information from the graphic without requiring explanation from the text. The Organizing Information chapter includes a discussion of organizational strategies for various types of information. These strategies can be used to organize your own material, as well as assess the quality of your resources.

questions to ask about the content

- What is the subject? Is it consistent with the title of the document or resource?
- Is the information free from grammatical, typographical, and punctuation errors?
- Are the assumptions, the flow of information, and the conclusions logical?
- Are the visual aids accurate?
- Are facts and statements justified and supported with sound research or primary sources?
- Can the references be verified?
- Do the statements agree with what is generally accepted as being true?
- Is the information complete, or are data missing that, if provided, might change the interpretation of the document or resource?
- For digital information, is the information available in another format, such as a printed product in a library?

SELF-ASSESSMENT QUESTIONS

- What impact does lack of editing (demonstrated by typographical and grammatical errors) have on the information you read?
- What impact does an illogical arrangement of information have on the resources you use?

In addition to the actual content, copyright issues must have been addressed and dealt with legally and ethically. More will be said on this in the chapter about the ethical and legal issues surrounding information.

questions to ask about evaluating quality

- Is the information presented in a logical manner?
- Is the presentation consistent?
- Do the visual aids help to comprehend the material?
- Can the visual aids stand alone?

CASE IN POINT: NUTRITIONAL VALUE

Sheryl Fraser is a medical assistant working for a large physician practice. Her supervisor has asked her to develop some nutrition pamphlets to hand out to patients, encouraging them to change poor eating behaviors in favor of a diet within recommended dietary guidelines. The nutrition books in the office are outdated, so Sheryl decides to seek the needed information on the Internet. She types the search term "nutrition" using Google—which indicates about 412,000,000 results.

As she looks through the first few sites, she finds contradictory information. One site suggests eating a 10-day diet of grapefruit to lose weight rapidly. Another site recommends a high-protein, low-carbohydrate diet. A third site informs her that the only way to be healthy is to avoid all meat and dairy products and adhere to a vegetarian diet. Though Sheryl did learn basic nutrition principles in her training as a medical assistant, she wants to be able to refer to credible sources to support the information in her pamphlet.

- How will Sheryl begin to sort through the vast number of websites devoted to nutrition?
- Realizing the contradictory information on nutrition presented on the Internet, how will Sheryl determine which information is credible and which is not?
- How well do you think Sheryl will be able to judge which information she finds is accurate and which is inaccurate?
- How will Sheryl find data she can translate into information that her patients will understand, knowing that most of her patients have limited backgrounds in health-related topics, especially nutrition?

EVALUATING WEB SOURCES

You can find just about anything you want on the Internet: scholarly resources, full-text documents, directories, virtual libraries, university websites, academic research, portals, silly and joke sites, advertisements, trade sites, scams, personal pages, illegal activities, music, videos, and about anything else you can dream of. On the one hand, some of this information is excellent—reliable, verifiable, accurate, credible, and legal. On the other hand, much of the information on the Internet is not useful or appropriate—inaccurate, false, slanted, and sometimes illegal. Unfortunately, telling the difference from appearances alone can be difficult. The information-literate individual must know how to distinguish the good content from the bad. Train yourself to view web resources critically, even to the point of taking on a suspicious attitude toward each site you visit. This attitude will keep you critically analyzing the information that you find.

PUT IT TO USE Do not accept everything you read just because it is found online. Anyone can write and post anything for any purpose on the Internet.

EVALUATING WEBSITE AUTHORITY

When evaluating authority for websites, the three most important criteria to examine are author, owner or sponsor, and web address.

Author

As you have learned, in many information sources, the author's name is displayed prominently—on the front and title page of a book, on the first page of journal articles, and as a byline of newspaper and magazine articles.

When using websites, finding the author may take a bit more effort. A website is created for a specific purpose. For example, some websites sell products or services. Others convey information on a narrow topic area. Others attempt to persuade readers to adopt

CRITICAL THINKING QUESTIONS

- Conduct an online search for a topic in your field of study. What is an example of a website that has each of the following goals?
  - Selling a product or service
  - Informing readers of objective facts
  - Persuading readers to a specific way of thinking or supporting one side of an issue
- How did you determine the goal of each site?

a specific viewpoint or opinion. Still other sites are intended for entertainment. Some webpages are even created to damage another individual or group. With this in mind, you can gain a great deal of information on the credibility of a website by determining the authorship or the person or organization that created and maintains the site. You must think critically about the purpose of the site. Holding the author or owner of a website to the same standard as that of an author of a printed document is a vital part of determining his or her credibility.

In some cases, especially on reputable websites, information about the author is easily found on the website itself. Look for "Contact Us," "About," "Background," "Philosophy," "Who Am I?", or "Biography" on the site. Most websites give names, addresses, phone numbers, or email addresses inviting you to contact the site's owner or administrator. The goal is to try to find someone who is responsible for the site in terms of the information and its accuracy.

Sponsor or Owner

On a website, in addition to "About Us" or "Home," look at the header or footer for a distinctive watermark or branding on the page to find information about the sponsor or owner. Try to determine if sponsors or owners are stable and durable, indicating that they are reliable and will be around for the long term. A large professional organization tends to be more stable and durable than an individual. A Universal Resource Locator (URL) ending in .edu designates that the sponsorship is an academic institution. A URL ending in .gov indicates that the sponsor is a government agency. These sources are likely to be more credible than commercial or organizational sites. Keep in mind that anyone can publish anything on the Internet and websites can be taken down at any time. Also, look to see if you can contact the webmaster of the site. If you need help locating the owner of a website, you can search for the domain on www.whois.net to find out information about them.

WEB ADDRESS

Some information found on a website gives clues about the author, publisher, and sponsor or owner. By understanding the clues, you can more readily make an informed decision about the quality of the information and the site itself. Figure 4-3 provides a fictitious URL that serves as the example for the following discussion.

In our example, the top-level domain name is .edu, meaning that the server resides at an academic institution. The Internet Corporation for Assigned Names and Numbers (ICANN) is the entity responsible for approving these accredited top-level domains. Figure 4-4 provides a partial list of other common types of server locations that you should know.

ICANN continues to add accredited domain-name registrars to its top-level domains list in order to meet the demand created by business growth and technology advancement. In addition, each country has its own two-letter code that often is used in conjunction with the top-level domain name. For a complete list of country codes, go to the International Organization for Standardization (ISO) (www.iso.org). As examples, the ISO code for the United Kingdom is .uk and the ISO code for Botswana is .bw. When the ISO is used in the domain name, it signifies that the server is located in that country.

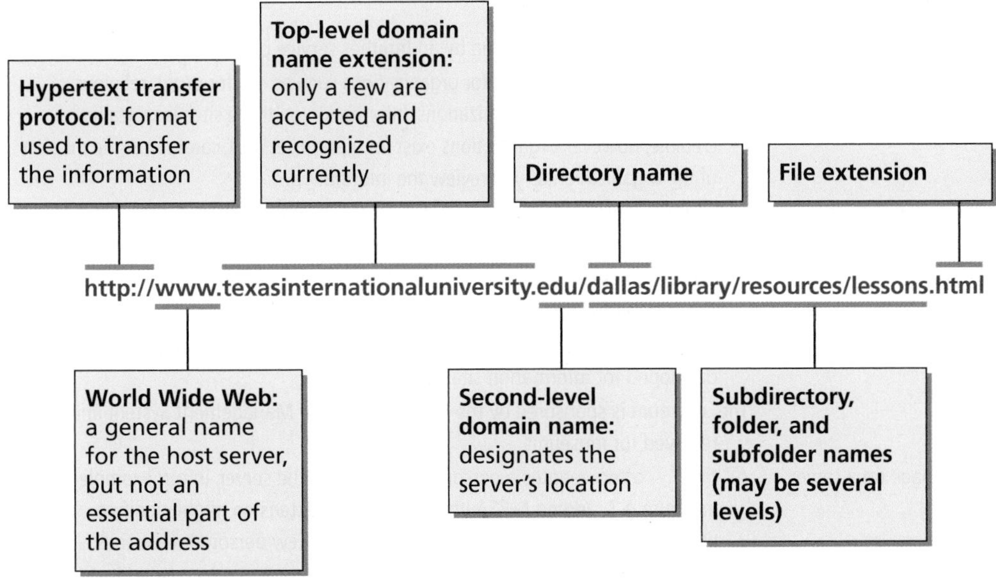

Figure 4-3 Fictitious Web Address.

4

PUT IT TO USE Typically, you can rely on the .gov and .edu sites as being reliable and presenting relatively accurate information. The government or educational entity behind the site usually is bound by a code of ethics and is watched by many different individuals or agencies. The other top-level domain name extensions may not afford the same level of confidence because these may have vested interests or may be created by individuals who have personal or organizational agendas.

4

Extension	Type of Organization	Description
.edu	Educational institution	The .edu extension tells that the website is sponsored by an educational institution, usually a college or university. These sites are often more reliable and credible than commercial or personal websites.
.com	Commercial organization	The .com extension tells that the website is a commercial site. These sites typically give information about a company, promote and advertise the company's products and services, and sometimes allow for online purchasing. The information is typically reliable, but is not scholarly.
.gov	Government agency	The .gov extension is reserved for governmental agencies and owned by the United States Federal Government. The information on these sites is typically viewed as credible.
.mil	Military entities	The .mil extension is reserved for military entities—Army, Navy, Air Force, Marines, and so forth.
.net	Internet service providers	The .net extension is sponsored by an Internet service provider.
.org	Organizations	The .org extension is reserved for organizations such as not-for-profit, religious, lobby, and charitable organizations. Information on these sites is typically credible; however, organizations exist for a purpose. Look carefully at the mission of the organization as you review the information.
.aero	Air transportation industry	The .aero extension is sponsored by the air transportation industry.
.biz	Businesses	The .biz extension is reserved for large and small businesses.
.coop	Cooperatives	The .coop extension is sponsored by the National Cooperative Business Association (NCBA) for cooperatives.
.info	Information	The .info extension is sponsored by the Afilias Global Registry Services and developed for information sites.
.museum	Museums	The .museum is sponsored by the Museum Domain Management System and is reserved for museums.
~	Personal webpage on a server	A "tilde" ~ often denotes a personal webpage on the server. In our example in Figure 4-3, adding /~BSmith after the .edu extension might signify a professor's personal website on this server. Review personal webpages carefully, as they may not be monitored as closely as pages created for institutions or departments of institutions.

Figure 4-4 URL Extensions.

EVALUATING WEBSITE CURRENCY

The currency of a website is critical if you plan to use that site as a resource in your research. On websites, the date of the last revision often is found on the bottom of the first page. A reputable website typically gives the last date the site was updated.

In some cases, each page includes a date, indicating the currency of the information. For example, if an organization's website has a page for the Board of Directors and the page has a recent date, you can assume with some certainty that the posted statements are current. Although not true in every case, a recent date usually is an indicator of currency, but be aware that a site could indicate an update and still contain outdated information.

Obviously, not all information requires the same attention to currency. A website pertaining to the ancient history of Greece does not require the same currency as a site that provides the latest state regulations on Medicare and Medicaid. A site that provides state regulations on Medicare and Medicaid from 1997 is of little use except for historical reference. In some cases, you might want the information posted on the site near the time the incident actually occurred. News websites often archive their periodicals so that you can see the stories as they were written at the time.

Website Stability

Unlike a print product, a website can be changed in a moment, and viewers may or may not be informed of the changes. The site can even be moved to a different web address with no forwarding information, making it difficult to locate, or deleted from the Internet altogether. A good clue to determine the stability of the site typically lies in the sponsorship. A nationally recognized organization (e.g., American Red Cross), a governmental agency, an academic institution (e.g., a college or university), or a large corporation (e.g., Chevron) is probably not going anywhere—at least not without making national news. These types of websites can usually be relied upon to remain stable. The consequences of an established organization's moving its website can be significant. Conversely, an individual's personal website might move with little or no serious repercussions.

Critical Thinking Questions

- Suppose an article you read suggests an information source from the Internet. You want to verify the facts by going to that information source, but the webpage had been discontinued. What will you do?
- What will you want the author of that content to have done to help you in your research?
- What kinds of issues might cause a website to be ignored or deleted from the Internet?

4

Keep in mind that a regular registration fee is required to maintain ownership of the web address, and some time and effort to maintain the site itself. Clues to websites that are not maintained include broken or dead links (links that do not go to the intended site), outdated links (links that go to old rather than new information), and information that does not match other resources you have determined to be current.

PUT IT TO USE Although you cannot be guaranteed that any site is stable and will be there when you want to return to it, it is best to try to use information from relatively stable sources. When you cite your references in a document and someone wants to review your sources of information, you may run into difficulties if the site you have referenced is no longer accessible.

EVALUATING WEBSITE CONTENT

Many websites have host advertisements to support the website. Although the presence of advertising does not negate the credibility of the information, it should cause you to take notice. Evaluate the advertisements carefully to determine if the relationship with the products or services being advertised influences the objectivity of the information. On webpages, advertising should be clearly separate from objective material. Websites should be straightforward, clearly differentiating advertisements from objective facts or statements.

Tips for recognizing biased content:

- excessive claims of certainty
- appeal to emotion
- personal attacks
- too good to be true
- something for sale
- associated cost or fee
- unsupported claims of fact

- ignoring or omitting contradictory facts or views
- appeals to popular opinion
- before-and-after testimonials
- suggestive or negative innuendos
- magnification or minimization of problems
- presentation of information out of context
- sarcastic or angry tone
- advertisements

EVALUATING MULTIMEDIA

So far, our focus has been on evaluating print and Internet resources. Multimedia resources include graphics, video resources, audio resources, simulations, animations, clip art, photographs, podcasts, vodcasts, and software. These resources can provide valuable information in an interesting delivery format. As with print and Internet resources, however, this type of information must be examined critically to determine if it is appropriate, credible, and useful for your purposes.

All information should be assessed in a similar way, regardless of how it is delivered or presented. Apply the same criteria as you would for a print or an Internet resource.

1. Evaluate the resource.
2. Evaluate the authority.
3. Evaluate the currency of the resource and information.
4. Evaluate the content itself.

Additional criteria for evaluating multimedia resources include the following:

- **FUNCTIONALITY.** How well do multimedia work within the environment in which they are being viewed? For many multimedia choices, technical aspects determine how or if the information can be viewed. If viewing multimedia from a Blu-ray, CD, or DVD, the application should work without error on the computer. Multimedia viewed on the Internet should load relatively quickly and should state clearly if any additional plug-ins or software is needed for viewing. For Internet multimedia, viewers often are required to download a special application, such as QuickTime, Java, ActiveX, or Acrobat Reader. In most cases, these plug-ins are free and easily accessible on the Internet. A good website has a link to the pages where the software can be downloaded.

- **USABILITY.** Usability means that the multimedia are easy to use or "user friendly." This criterion is especially notable with software, animations, simulations, audio objects, and video objects. Layout should be logical and consistent throughout the object. The navigation should be intuitive and easy to find and follow. Any instructions should be clear and complete. Links should be functional, and if they are not, there should be a mechanism for reporting nonfunctional links to a webmaster.

  Multimedia objects should download quickly, even at slower Internet speeds, and downloading instructions should be clear. If the tool is complicated, as with certain software, a Help tool should be available to answer common questions or provide instructions for all actions.

- **ACCESSIBILITY.** Many features make a multimedia object accessible to individuals who have various disabilities. An example of a design feature of a webpage is an ALT tag for links and images to assist sight-impaired viewers. A complete list of standards for accessible design can be found on the Americans with Disabilities Act website at www.ada.gov.

4

Critical Thinking Question

- What kinds of multimedia might be useful in your field? Give several examples of multimedia you might be required to evaluate.

success steps for evaluating multimedia resources

- Evaluate the resource.
- Evaluate the authority.
- Evaluate the currency.
- Evaluate the content.
- Evaluate the functionality.
- Evaluate the usability.
- Evaluate the accessibility.

CHAPTER SUMMARY

This chapter summarized how to evaluate information. You learned that information-literate individuals critically analyze information and its sources to ensure that it is useful. You also learned that while your evaluation is based in large part on common sense, several components should be reviewed to assess the quality of the information. These include evaluating the resource, evaluating the authority, and evaluating the currency of the information. Additionally, you learned that inspecting websites for authority, currency, and content is important to determine if the website is a credible source. Finally, you learned that it is equally as important to assess the information retrieved from a multimedia source as it is from print and Internet sources.

POINTS TO KEEP IN MIND

In this chapter, several main points were discussed in detail:

- Evaluating information using critical analysis applies to print materials and resources, multimedia resources, and information on the Internet.
- The publication timeline is one of the criteria for evaluating a resource.
- Journals and magazines are common sources of information. These include scholarly journals, trade publications, and popular magazines. Each of these forms has a different purpose and target audience.
- Evaluating the authority means to look critically at the author of the information, as well as the sponsor or owner of the specific resource, such as the publisher or owner of a website.
- Currency refers to the timeliness of the information. In a print product, this includes the date and edition of the publication. For websites, the date of the last revision is considered.

- When evaluating the content of the information, factors to take into account include the intended audience, the purpose and scope, the objectivity, the accuracy and verifiability, and the overall quality of the content.
- In addition to the criteria for evaluating information for print and Internet resources, multimedia adds functionality, usability, and accessibility to the list.

apply it

4

Activity #1: Information Checklist

GOAL:* *To review and organize the criteria for evaluating information and information sources, and to create a checklist for this evaluation.

STEP 1: Review the various criteria for evaluating information resources and the content.

STEP 2: Develop a checklist to ensure that you complete a thorough evaluation when you conduct your research.

Activity #2: Information Resource Comparison

GOAL:* *To emphasize the importance of understanding the type of resource, and how to evaluate credibility and timing.

STEP 1: Form a group with your classmates. Every person in the group should select one topic and then bring in one example of each of the following types of information sources:

a. a refereed scholarly journal

b. a trade publication

c. a popular magazine

STEP 2: Present your examples to the group and compare the characteristics of each that you would assess as you evaluate the resource.

Activity #3: Web Research

GOAL:* *To develop a full understanding of the various kinds of information found on the Internet.

STEP 1: Conduct a search to find examples of the following types of websites:

a. an excellent webpage that provides highly credible information

b. a questionable webpage that provides information for which you cannot easily determine the credibility

c. a webpage designed to sell you something

d. a webpage designed to influence your opinion on a controversial issue by using emotion and extreme remarks

e. a webpage designed as a hoax or to mislead purposely the reader for some aim

STEP 2: Print out a copy of each webpage, and clearly identify the characteristics that give you clues about the type of information the page provides.

SUGGESTED ITEMS FOR LEARNING PORTFOLIO

4

Refer to the "How to Use This Book" section at the beginning of this textbook for more information about learning portfolios.

- Checklist for Evaluating an Information Resource and Information
- List of information resources that are useful in your field of study, categorized by type of resources

REFERENCES

American Evaluation Association. (n.d.). *Welcome to the American Evaluation Association*. Retrieved June 13, 2013, from http://www.eval.org/

American Heart Association. (2013). *About Us: Our Mission*. Retrieved June 13, 2013, from http://www.heart.org/HEARTORG/

Pew Research Center. (2016). *About Pew Research Center*. Retrieved February 5, 2016, from http://www.pewresearch.org/

Rocketclips, Inc./Shutterstock.com

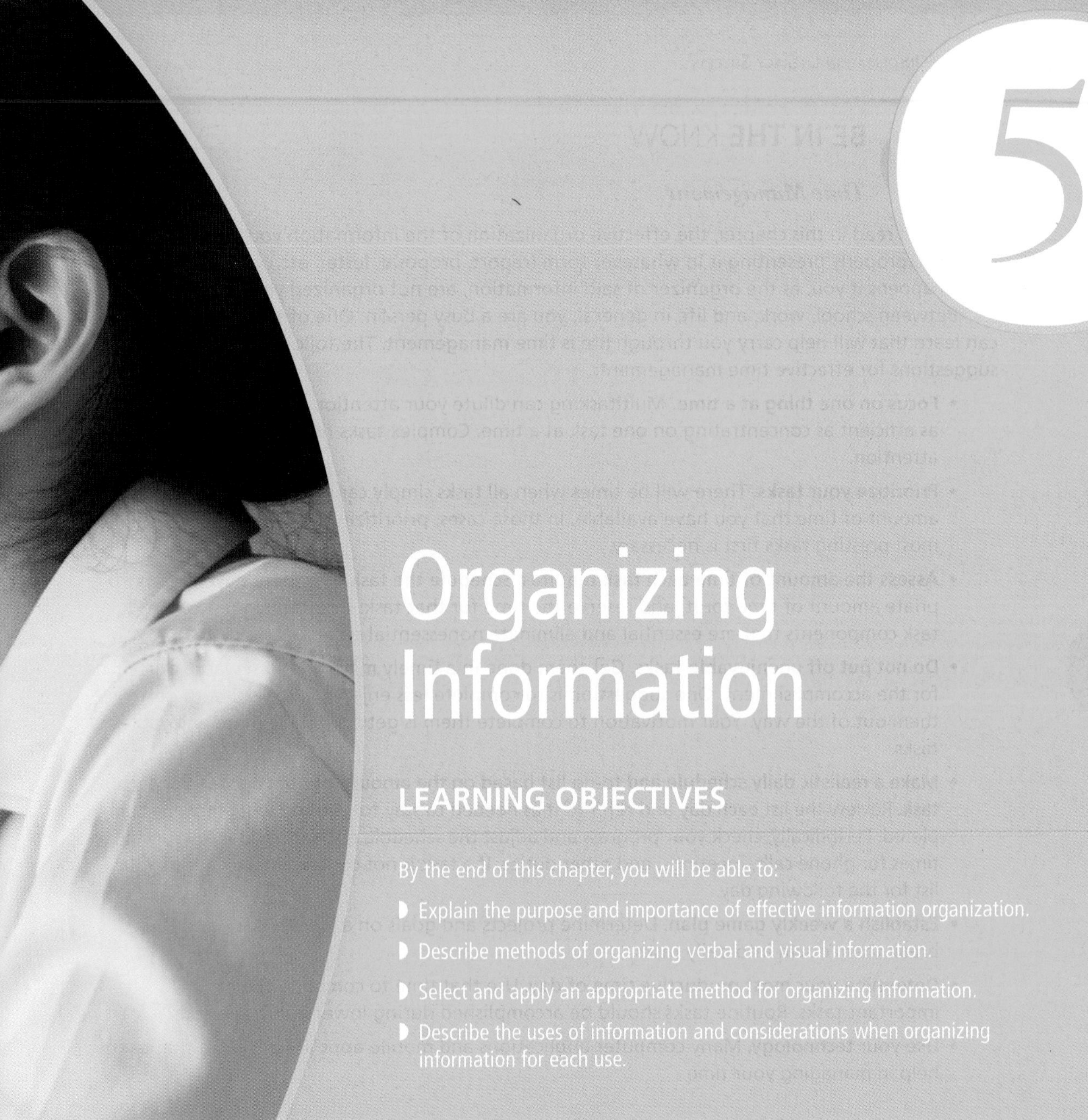

5

Organizing Information

LEARNING OBJECTIVES

By the end of this chapter, you will be able to:

- Explain the purpose and importance of effective information organization.
- Describe methods of organizing verbal and visual information.
- Select and apply an appropriate method for organizing information.
- Describe the uses of information and considerations when organizing information for each use.

BE IN THE KNOW

Time Management

As you will read in this chapter, the effective organization of the information you have found is critical to properly presenting it in whatever form (report, proposal, letter, etc.) you choose. But what happens if you, as the organizer of said information, are not organized yourself?

Between school, work, and life in general, you are a busy person. One of the best skills you can learn that will help carry you through life is time management. The following are some suggestions for effective time management:

- **Focus on one thing at a time.** Multitasking can dilute your attention and may not be as efficient as concentrating on one task at a time. Complex tasks require concentrated attention.
- **Prioritize your tasks.** There will be times when all tasks simply cannot be completed in the amount of time that you have available. In those cases, prioritizing and completing the most pressing tasks first is necessary.
- **Assess the amount of time each task requires.** Schedule the task when you have the appropriate amount of time for it, and reserve the time for that task. Determine the tasks and task components that are essential and eliminate nonessential elements.
- **Do not put off unenjoyable tasks.** Get them done in a timely manner and reward yourself for the accomplishment. One suggestion is to complete less enjoyable tasks first to get them out of the way. Your motivation to complete them is getting to the more enjoyable tasks.
- **Make a realistic daily schedule and to-do list based on the amount of time needed for each task.** Review the list each day and refer to it as needed to stay focused on what must be completed. Periodically, check your progress and adjust the schedule as needed. Identify specific times for phone calls, meetings, and other duties. If a task is not completed, move it to your list for the following day.
- **Establish a weekly game plan.** Determine projects and goals on a weekly basis and then break them down into daily tasks.
- **Determine your most productive time of day.** Use that time to complete the most important tasks. Routine tasks should be accomplished during lower-energy periods.
- **Use your technology.** Many computer applications and mobile apps are available that can help in managing your time.

SOLVING INFORMATION PROBLEMS: ORGANIZE THE INFORMATION

Step 4 of the research process involves organization, as shown in Figure 5-1. Many elements contribute to effective organization of information. The goal of your task will define whether you are preparing a proposal, a technical report, or some other type of presentation. Selecting the appropriate document and preparing it in a way that communicates your message and accomplishes your goal are critical to your success.

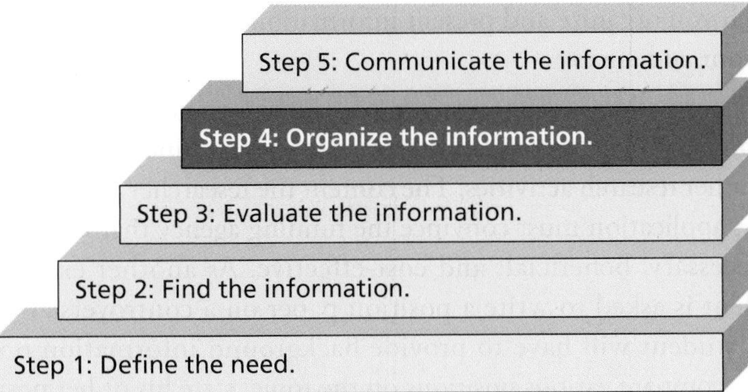

Figure 5-1 Research Process Step 4: Organize the Information. The fourth step of any research project should be to organize the information effectively.

Once you have determined the appropriate type of document, you must present your information in a logical and coherent manner that holds your audience members' attention and brings them to a logical conclusion. The way in which you organize facts and figures, as well as the format in which they are presented, largely determines the response you will receive.

This chapter will introduce you to organizational methods, as well as documents and other resources commonly used in professional settings that you may be asked to complete at some time in your career—proposals, technical reports, tables, charts, and multimedia. General concepts of organization will be applied to each, and considerations specific to each of the formats will be discussed. Many of the concepts presented here can be applied to other documents and reports that you may encounter.

THE IMPORTANCE OF EFFECTIVE ORGANIZATION OF INFORMATION

Think of a time when you were attempting to understand a piece of information or a document that was poorly organized. Recall the frustration and difficulty you might have felt as you attempted to sort

SELF-ASSESSMENT QUESTIONS

- Based on your experience, what is an example that demonstrates effective organization of information?
- Compare that example with an example of ineffective organization of information. What are the differences between the two situations?
- How could the example of ineffective organization be improved upon?

5

through and use it. Compare that situation to a time when you used material that was organized methodically and efficiently. Chances are that you experienced less stress, used your time more efficiently, and completed your task more easily and effectively. The manner in which you organize and present information can have the same effect on your audiences.

Information is usually presented to achieve a goal. For example, a researcher who is applying for a grant is seeking funding to complete his or her research activities. The content the researcher presents in the grant application must convince the funding agency that the research is necessary, beneficial, and cost-effective. As another example, a student is asked to write a position paper on a controversial topic. The student will have to provide background information on the issue, compare various positions on the topic, state his or her position with supporting reasoning and explanation, and draw a conclusion. The goal for each of these projects calls for different organizational strategies.

Effectively organized information allows you to be understood, and for the recipient to apply, question, or utilize what you have presented. Material that is arranged and presented effectively contributes to productive communication. Productivity on the job also is facilitated by effective organization of information. Reports, proposals, and other documents that clearly communicate relevant facts contribute to efficient completion of tasks and projects. Well-organized information in professional reports and presentations will contribute to the success of your organization as well as your professional development and advancement.

ORGANIZATIONAL STRATEGIES

You are more likely to be understood when you organize your information and communication effectively. Material that is organized in a logical and meaningful fashion is more readily used and applied than random, disorganized data (Huitt, 2003). By arranging information systematically, you will maximize the opportunity for your audience to receive an accurate message. For example, a criminal justice student who is describing the events leading up to a crime might choose to arrange them chronologically because this type of organization best conveys the sequence of events leading to the crime. If the same student wants to explore the motives for the crime, however, the information might be organized according to possible cause and effect.

As a presenter, you have choices in how the content is arranged. Huitt (2003), an educational psychologist, discusses the organization of information as it pertains to learning. On the other hand, Wurman (2000), a graphic designer and architect, as well as Stucker (2006), a consultant and entrepreneur, approach the organization of information from an applied perspective. Although the focus of their work differs, each has been very successful in conveying methods for improving organizational skills to their readers and audiences. Consider the following strategies, which are based on the work of these three researchers.

PUT IT TO USE Consider the goal you wish to achieve by presenting your information. Organize this information in a way that will logically lead to your goal. Explore *concept mapping* and *mind mapping* by completing an Internet search using these as your search terms. Consider how mind or concept mapping can help you organize your information.

ORGANIZATION BY CATEGORY OR CONCEPT

Separate ideas that combine to produce a concept must be understood individually before their synthesis makes sense. This calls for organization by category or concept. For example, if a student of early childhood education wants to describe a positive classroom environment for kindergarten students, she first might discuss the physical classroom environment, types of activities available to the children, characteristics of the teacher, and a schedule appropriate for this age group. Each element of the positive classroom is discussed in terms of its attributes, why these attributes are important for kindergartners, and techniques for developing each attribute in the classroom. She then pulls together the individual elements and describes a typical day in the kindergarten class. The discussion includes how the separate concepts blend and interact to produce a positive classroom environment. Effectively organized information has provided a clear description of each element and enabled the audience to synthesize them into a coherent concept.

Organization by category or concept also is effective when constructing a case to support a premise. Consider the example of a student in a healthcare management class who is involved in a debate over private versus government-sponsored health insurance coverage. In this example, the student is promoting government-sponsored health programs. He discusses individual themes, such as the financial burden of illness and uninsured individuals, the cost-effectiveness of implementing preventive health measures, strategies for implementing government-sponsored programs, and the importance of implementing and maintaining electronic health records (EHR). He supports his statements with reliable data that he has researched and evaluated for credibility. The student then brings together his ideas to provide a convincing case for a government-sponsored health program. In this scenario, well-organized information makes the student's case more compelling. Both of these examples use the synthesis of ideas to create a concept.

A variation on organization by concept is to begin with a major concept and break it down into the elements that form the central idea. Continuing with the example of the early childhood education student, consider that she is presenting information on playground-management strategies. In this example, playground management is the major concept. Within that concept, she might talk about setting behavior expectations appropriate to kindergartners, structuring group activities, and safety considerations. This application of organization by concept uses analysis of a concept by breaking it down into its respective parts.

CRITICAL THINKING QUESTIONS

- What information in your field would be organized most effectively by concept or category? Would you organize this information using synthesis or analysis strategies? Why?
- Consider a presentation or assignment that you completed recently. How did you implement the concepts? How might you have implemented them further to improve your presentation or assignment?
- Consider an assignment that you currently are completing or will be starting in the near future. How can you implement organization by category or concept to benefit the assignment? Conversely, why might this method not be appropriate for this assignment?

5

CHRONOLOGICAL ORGANIZATION

Organization according to time, called chronological organization, is used when the sequence of events influences an outcome. A common example is found in the instructions for assembling something such as a model or a piece of furniture. Information provided out of sequence would lead to failure and frustration. And consider the example of a computer technology student who, in a practical exam, is explaining and demonstrating the steps involved in repairing a computer.

To be successful, the steps must be explained and executed in a specific sequence. Likewise, the allied health student who is describing or demonstrating a treatment procedure must arrange the information in the proper sequence or the treatment is likely to be ineffective.

Often, chronological organization is necessary for a sequence of events to make sense and explain an outcome. Consider how effective your next joke would be if you were to give the punch line first and then tell the details of the joke! The example of the criminology student describing the events leading to a crime provides an example of effectively leading to and explaining an outcome using chronological organization.

Certain information that is sequenced chronologically involves transition from one phase to the next. In these situations, recipients of the information have to understand the progression between steps or stages. For example, a physical therapy assistant student describing the progression of a patient through treatment must arrange treatment steps in sequence and also must clarify the relationship of one phase of treatment to the next.

In another example, the student in a human development class is describing the sequence of development in an infant. The developmental stages must be described sequentially, and the information organized and explained to demonstrate the continuity of development. Each of these cases illustrates the importance of information that explains the relationship between the chronological phases.

HIERARCHICAL ORGANIZATION

Hierarchical organization is used when information is best conveyed in a specific order, such as from most to least important or least complex to most complex. Bloom's taxonomy, which you first read about in the Introduction to Information Literacy chapter, is an example of a hierarchical arrangement beginning with the least complex concepts and progressing to the most complex. Another example is the computer technology student who is describing the process of troubleshooting a computer problem. He starts by looking for simple problems, such as a poorly connected cable, and describes progressing to more complex problems, such as examining the processor. A graphic design student uses hierarchical organization when she creates a brochure for a product and lists the various models of the product, beginning with the model

CRITICAL THINKING QUESTIONS

- What information in your field would be most effectively organized chronologically? How would you include transitional information?
- Consider a presentation or an assignment that you recently completed. How did you implement these concepts? How might you have implemented them further to improve your presentation or assignment?
- Consider an assignment that you are currently completing or will be starting in the near future. How might you implement chronological organization to benefit this assignment? Conversely, why might this organization not be effective for this assignment?

that has the fewest features and lowest cost and progressing to the model with the most features and highest cost.

ALPHABETICAL ORGANIZATION

Obvious examples of alphabetical organization are dictionaries and contact lists. Alphabetical organization is appropriate when the reader knows the information he or she is looking for and must locate it by a keyword. Glossaries and directories are additional examples of resources in which alphabetical organization is effective and appropriate.

In some circumstances, you will be presenting pieces of information as equivalent and nonhierarchical in nature. Presenting the material alphabetically is a method of organization that does not imply any type of order based on attribute or characteristic. For instance, if you are crediting individuals who contributed to a project, listing them alphabetically avoids the implication that one individual contributed more than another. Or consider the pharmacy technician student who is describing, as part of an assignment, the characteristics of various medications. By ordering the medications alphabetically, the student avoids any implied hierarchy. They also make the list user-friendly because the names of the medications are easily located alphabetically.

Critical Thinking Questions

- What information in your field would be most effectively organized hierarchically?
- What information in your field would be organized most effectively alphabetically?
- Consider a presentation or an assignment that you recently completed. How did you implement these concepts? How might you have implemented them further to improve your presentation or assignment?
- Consider an assignment that you are currently completing or will be starting in the near future. How might you implement a hierarchical organization to benefit this assignment? Conversely, why might hierarchical organization be ineffective for this assignment? How can you implement an alphabetical organization to benefit the assignment? Conversely, why might it not be appropriate for this assignment?

5

questions to ask to select a method of organizing information

- What am I trying to accomplish by presenting this information? What is my goal?
- What organizational method best supports my goal?
- Is my information best organized according to ideas or concepts that build to a logical conclusion?
- Is my information best organized according to time or in a sequential order?
- Is my information best organized in a hierarchical fashion to show the relative importance of the information pieces?
- Is my information best located by a keyword or inappropriate for hierarchical organization?

Table 5-1 summarizes the strategies discussed for organizing information. Table 5-2 reviews and summarizes Bloom's concepts and suggests how each level of the taxonomy can be used to guide the information-organization process. Keep these concepts in mind, as the organizational strategies discussed here will be described according to Bloom's taxonomy.

TABLE 5-1 SUMMARY OF INFORMATION ORGANIZATION STRATEGIES

Organization Method	Description
Organization by category or concept	Separate ideas are combined to produce a concept. The synthesis of individual ideas produces a logical conclusion. Conversely, a concept can be presented in its entirety and subsequently analyzed into its parts.
Chronological organization	Chronological organization is organization according to time. The sequence of events influences or explains an outcome.
Hierarchical organization	Hierarchical organization is used when information is best conveyed based on its importance. It indicates the relative significance of information, such as from most to least important or from least complex to most complex.
Alphabetical organization	Alphabetical organization is appropriate when the reader knows the information he or she is looking for and has to locate it by a keyword. It is used to organize information in a manner that does not suggest a hierarchy.

TABLE 5-2 APPLYING BLOOM'S TAXONOMY AS A STRATEGY FOR ORGANIZING INFORMATION

Bloom's Level	Definition	Uses
Knowledge	Provides facts and figures	Presenting factual background information, often as a foundation for more complex ideas
Comprehension	Compares, summarizes, and shows an understanding of concepts	Providing examples and explanations of facts and background information
Application	Relates an example or a set of rules to an authentic situation	Explaining how something is done; applying a procedure to a set of circumstances
Analysis	Breaks down a concept into its components	Simplifying a complex concept; showing the components of a complex idea
Synthesis	Creates a new idea or concept from single facts or components	Presenting a new idea; explaining how individual elements combine to create a new concept
Evaluation	Makes a judgment about the effectiveness or appropriateness of an idea or concept	Defending or advocating a position or idea; presenting a solution

5

CASE IN POINT: REPORT IT

Anna Hensley graduated from college six months ago. Recently she accepted a position as a research assistant for a human resources firm, where her duties include accessing, organizing, and presenting information on hiring trends, salaries, industry growth, and other topics related to the human resources field. She also is responsible for preparing funding proposals for various projects. Anna must be able to locate relevant information, organize it logically into a document appropriate to her purpose, and present it effectively.

During her orientation period she was guided by her supervisor's expertise. Now Anna has received the first major project to complete independently. Although she is adept at locating and collecting information that supports her research goals, she is less sure of her ability to arrange and present it effectively. She is concerned about selecting the appropriate type of report or document, what information to include, how to organize it, and how to present it in a way that her audience will understand and that will achieve the project goals.

- How familiar are you with various types of documents and reports and their uses?
- For each type of document or report, how logically could you organize the information?
- How would you go about selecting an organizational plan?
- How would you select your presentation method? When would you use a verbal format? When would you use a visual format? When would you consider other media?
- If you decide to use a table or chart, how would you present its content logically and clearly?
- If you choose to use presentation software (such as Microsoft PowerPoint), what considerations would you make during preparation and which features of the application are you likely to use?

PRESENTING INFORMATION EFFECTIVELY

Information can be presented verbally (orally or written), graphically, or through multimedia. Your choice of presentation media depends on several factors including your audience, the type of information you are conveying, and the presentation environment. Regardless of the choice you make, be sure to keep the following considerations in mind.

- **Organization of the presentation.** The visual organization of your presentation is as important as the way in which the information itself is structured. For example, written documents must be formatted to maximize legibility. Graphics and multimedia must be easy to see and clearly understand. Electronic information, such as that presented on webpages, must be navigated intuitively.
- **Ethical and legal considerations.** All information must be referenced properly and the sources cited. Information must be used in a way that applies it rather than simply repeats someone else's work. Plagiarism is illegal and unethical in all presentation formats. (Plagiarism and appropriate referencing will be addressed in the Legal and Ethical Issues Related to Information chapter.)
- **Credibility considerations.** Information must come from credible, current, and reliable sources. Apply the evaluation methods discussed throughout this text to all information used in any presentation.

aerogondo2/Shutterstock

Selecting your presentation medium carefully will maximize the effectiveness of your information

questions to ask to present information effectively

- Who is my audience?
- What is the purpose of my presentation?
- What is the presentation environment?
- Does the organization of my presentation maximize its legibility?
- Are my information sources properly cited and referenced?
- Have I ensured that my information comes from current, credible, and reliable sources?

5

ORGANIZING WRITTEN DOCUMENTS

Written presentations include documents such as reports, proposals, needs assessments, and others. As part of effective organization, written work must be presented professionally and in a manner that reflects the standards of your field.

The first step in creating an effective document or presentation is to organize the information in a way in which you can use it. After you have implemented your research strategy, you are likely to have an extensive amount of material. Arranging the material in a way that is useful to you provides the foundation for creating an effective end product. Consider the following suggestions for organizing the information that you have retrieved. You may find that a combination of these strategies will best meet your needs.

PUT IT TO USE While researching information, implement a method or methods for organizing your data that fits your style and preferences.

- **Know the organization strategy you have selected.** Understanding how you are going to arrange your information will allow you to organize your sources accordingly. For example, if you have decided that chronological organization is most appropriate for your topic, you can sort your sources in an accurate sequence. If you are organizing information by concept, you may choose to sort your data into folders labeled for each main idea.
- **Use a format that works for you.** Do you find yourself buried in piles of paper on your desk? Do you cringe at the thought of reading documents on the computer screen? Collect your resources in a format that works for you. Some individuals read printed copies more effectively and benefit from taking notes on them, highlighting important points. Other people prefer to read documents electronically and take brief notes as they read from the computer screen. Be aware, though, that some information may be available in only one format, so you will have to be flexible. For example, if some of your material is available only in a book and you prefer the electronic documents, you will have to adapt your preferred method to that format.

- **Use a cataloging system that works for you.** A cataloging system is the system you use to physically organize material. Examples of cataloging systems are note cards, binders, electronic folders, and various types of files. Each has its advantages and shortcomings. For example, individual file folders allow you to easily separate documents into categories that support individual concepts. Your choice will depend on your personal preference and style. Table 5-3, which follows, summarizes the advantages and disadvantages of various cataloging systems and gives suggestions for using each.

The manner in which a document is prepared contributes to its organization. Compare a document that uses graphics effectively to a document that uses graphics randomly and haphazardly. Thoughtful and effectively placed graphics add to the clarity and meaning of the document, whereas misused graphics can distract and confuse the reader. Consider the following factors when preparing written documents.

- **Follow the recommended style.** Guidelines for writing style come from various sources. Style guides such as *The Chicago Manual of Style*, *Publication Manual of the American Psychological Association (APA)*, and the *Modern Language Association (MLA) Style Manual* provide standards for language use and citation of references. Each profession and field tends to adopt one style consistently. For example, the social science fields generally use the APA style in research papers and journal articles. Preparing and organizing documents in the style used in your field provides readers with a recognized format. Style guides also provide consistent formatting elements such as spacing, margins, treatment of graphics, tables, charts, and other elements. Consistent formatting allows the reader to recognize and locate information more easily.
- **Use language and level of complexity appropriate to your audience.** As much as possible, know who will be reading your finished document or listening to your presentation. For general audiences, use simple language and define terms when necessary. For professional audiences or groups with more advanced knowledge, use more technical language and terminology. Choosing the level of language appropriate to your audience is related closely to selecting an appropriate level of resources for the type of project you are completing. For general audiences,

TABLE 5-3 INFORMATION CATALOGING SYSTEMS.

Some of the more commonly used techniques for cataloging information are summarized here, and you may be aware of others.

Cataloging System	Advantages	Disadvantages	Suggested Uses
Note cards	• Convenient for recording one idea or fact per card. • Small size allows opportunity to sort and rearrange information. Note card apps are available for use on a computer or mobile device.	• Numerous cards can be difficult to manage.	• Arrange events chronologically. • Arrange information hierarchically. • Arrange information alphabetically. • Elaborate on a single idea or concept per card to effectively organize information.
Binders	• Documents can be stored and reviewed in original form. • All information is kept in one place. • Addition of divider tabs allows efficient organization of information.	• Sorting information by individual facts is more difficult in full document form.	• Create a section of information for each concept or idea.
Electronic folders	• Use of paper is minimized. • Information can be retrieved and reorganized with relative ease.	• May not be readily accessible without a computer. • If documents are bookmarked, will require Internet access.	• Sort information by concept or idea. • Rearrange and duplicate information to meet a different need.
Individual file folders	• Documents can be stored and reviewed in original form. • Information can be easily rearranged as needed and to serve various purposes.	• Can be challenging to keep multiple individual folders together.	• Create a folder for each idea or concept. • Create a separate folder for a designated time period, and organize information chronologically.
Expandable files	• Documents can be stored and reviewed in original form. • Information can be kept in one place.	• Can be bulky.	• Use in ways similar to individual files.
Visual organizers	• Effective for visual and kinesthetic learners. • Information can be easily rearranged. • Provides a view of the "big picture."	• Not easily transported. • May be less effective for verbal learners. • Difficult to include in-depth detail.	• Show relationships between concepts. • Create as a timeline.

you are more likely to use language and organizational strategies based on the less complex levels of Bloom's taxonomy, for example, and with more seasoned professionals, organization based on more advanced levels of the taxonomy is appropriate.

You probably will agree that a presentation for new graduates should be more basic than a presentation for seasoned professionals. New members of a profession tend to need straightforward facts and figures as they learn about the field. Facts, examples, and other information that provide a foundation for learning are appropriate for individuals who are learning about a field. Based on Bloom's taxonomy, you would organize your information according to the lower levels of thinking and use the knowledge, comprehension, and possibly application levels.

More advanced members of the profession can be expected to have the foundational knowledge and to be using it to assess situations, solve problems creatively, and evaluate circumstances. For these professionals, you likely would organize information based on the higher levels of Bloom's taxonomy—analysis, synthesis, and evaluation. As might be expected, more experienced professionals are able to use it in a more complex manner. Thus, you can use Bloom's taxonomy to organize information differently, in a way that meets the needs of your audience.

Language use also must be considered in terms of your audience. If you use highly technical language, you probably will lose an audience of people who are inexperienced in your field. Consider the example of a physician explaining a complex medical issue to a patient. Unless the patient is a medical professional with the appropriate background, the physician will have to use nontechnical language that the patient knows if he or she is to understand and comply with treatment. Conversely, language that is too simple may not hold the interest of a more knowledgeable audience and may be insulting to their level of expertise. The following are guidelines for organizing a presentation to communicate effectively to a specific audience.

- **Organize information from simple to complex.** Organizing information from simple to complex provides a foundation on which the recipient of it can build more complex concepts. Suppose you are teaching someone to drive. Before starting the ignition, you will provide basic information about the car, including where the various controls are located and activated; how to adjust the mirrors and seat; and how to steer, turn, and

CRITICAL THINKING QUESTIONS

Imagine that you are preparing to give two presentations. One will be for new graduates just getting started in your field, and the other will be for seasoned professionals.

- What differences would you make in the two presentations?
- How could you use Bloom's taxonomy to organize the information in each of the presentations?

use other factors in controlling the car. Next, you might ask the learner to review the information you have provided and repeat what you have described to indicate understanding. All of this is done before asking the new driver to actually drive the car.

After the learner has actually driven the car, you might ask him or her to compare the actual driving experience to what he or she thought it would be like and to consider how this insight will contribute to the learning experience. As the learner practices and further develops driving skills, you will ask him or her to solve problems commonly encountered on the road and to assess his or her progress. By organizing the information from simple to complex, you have led the learner from the basics of driving to being able to solve problems and to evaluate various driving situations. Table 5-4 illustrates how this example reflects Bloom's taxonomy.

5

TABLE 5-4 SIMPLE-TO-COMPLEX ORGANIZATION RELATED TO BLOOM'S TAXONOMY

Level in Bloom's Taxonomy	Step of Teaching How to Drive a Car	Explanation
Knowledge	The learner receives basic information about the car, such as where the controls are located; how to adjust the mirrors and seat; and how to steer, turn, and use other factors in controlling the car.	The new driver learns the facts that are foundational to maneuvering the car effectively and safely.
Comprehension	The learner reviews or summarizes the information provided and gives some examples.	The new driver translates the basic knowledge into his or her own words and, in doing so, explains and demonstrates an understanding of the concepts.
Application	The learner actually drives the car.	The new driver puts the newly learned concepts to use.
Analysis	The learner compares the actual driving experience to what he or she thought it would be like.	The new driver compares and contrasts the experience with his or her expectations, and assesses each element of the driving experience.
Synthesis	The learner considers how this insight will contribute to the learning experience. The learner solves problems commonly encountered on the road.	The new driver integrates what he or she has learned with his or her own ideas and develops new concepts about the driving experience. The learner combines concepts to formulate solutions to problems.
Evaluation	The learner assesses his or her progress.	The new driver compares his or her proficiency to acceptable standards of skill and safety and makes an assessment of the skills he or she needs to develop.

- **Follow conventional language, spelling, and grammar standards.** Professionals should avoid slang as well as unorthodox spelling and grammar. Using recognized language specifications contributes to the perception of well-organized information. Imagine that you were reading a document containing slang from the 1970s and 1980s. Although you might be entertained and amused, how seriously would you take the information? Of course, using an occasional slang word for emphasis can be an effective tool. Generally, however, language should follow standard guidelines. Guidelines for language conventions, as we said, can be found in the style guide (APA, MLA, etc.) used in your field. Finally, you should respect elements of diversity and incorporate them appropriately in the context of your document or presentation.
- **Check for accuracy.** In organizing information, you must ensure its accuracy to maximize its usefulness and minimize the chances of misquoting sources. Information that is clear and correct contributes to a well-received document or presentation and supports your credibility as an information provider.
- **Use graphics that are clear and enhance the content of the document.** Thoughtfully selected graphics and infographics can enhance the clarity of information, in contrast to randomly placed graphics, which detract from your message. When considering the use of graphics in the overall organization of your document or presentation, you first must consider how the graphics mesh with the written text.

PUT IT TO USE Use Bloom's taxonomy to determine the appropriate level of complexity of information for your audience. Generally, audiences with less experience will benefit from information structured at the lower levels of the taxonomy, while more experienced audiences are likely to benefit from information organized at the higher levels.

ORGANIZING GRAPHICS

Image Source RF/Cadalpe/Getty Images

Graphics should be clearly related to the information in the text, convey an accurate message, and effectively communicate without having to read the text.

Of the many types of graphics that can be used in documents and presentations, each has its advantages for conveying various kinds of information. Consider the following examples of graphics that are available:

- **Bar charts** (also called column charts or histograms) compare data by varying the length of the columns or bars. Bar charts can be drawn vertically or horizontally. Figure 5-2 provides an example of a bar chart. Variations of bar charts include simple column charts, stacked column charts, and 100 percent stacked bar charts. Electronic programs such as Microsoft Excel allow users to apply 3-D effects, color, labels, and legends to bar charts.

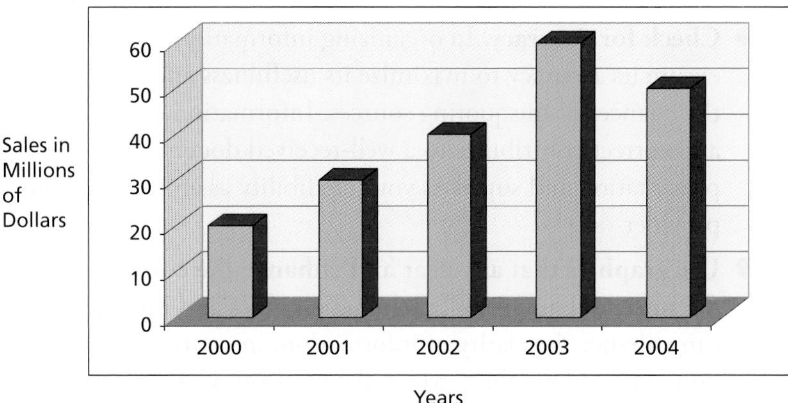

Figure 5-2 ***Example of a Bar Chart.*** This bar chart shows the sales of a company over the course of five years. By comparing the length of the bars, the reader can easily compare the sales between years.

- **Line charts** typically display a trend over time. Normally, time is represented on the x-axis of the graph and the element being measured over time is represented on the y-axis. Figure 5-3 is an example of a line chart. In addition to simple line charts, variations on line charts include stacked line charts and 100 percent stacked line charts. As in the case of bar charts, computer programs such as Microsoft Excel allow the user to apply 3-D effects, along with markers at each data point, color, and legends.

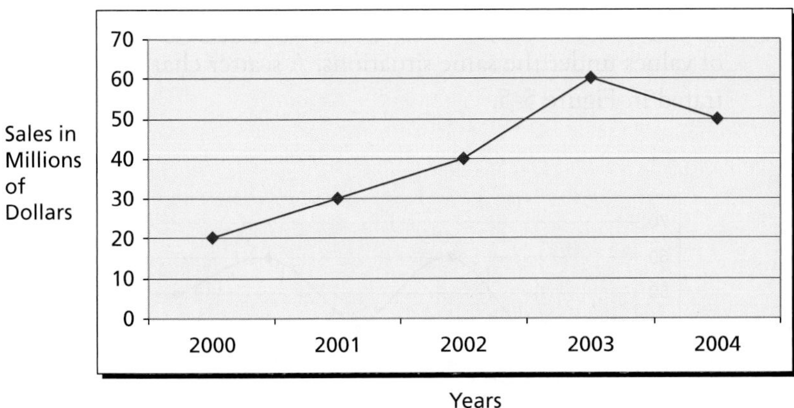

Figure 5-3 ***Example of a Line Chart.*** This line chart shows the same sales of the company represented in Figure 5-2. Instead of comparing the length of the bars, the line connecting the data points clearly indicates the trend over time.

- **Pie charts** show the contribution of each value to a total, allowing the reader to understand the relationship of parts to the whole. An example of a pie chart is provided in Figure 5-4. Types of pie charts include the simple pie chart, an exploded pie chart, and a bar of a pie chart. As with other types of charts, you can add 3-D effects, color, labels, and legends, as desired.

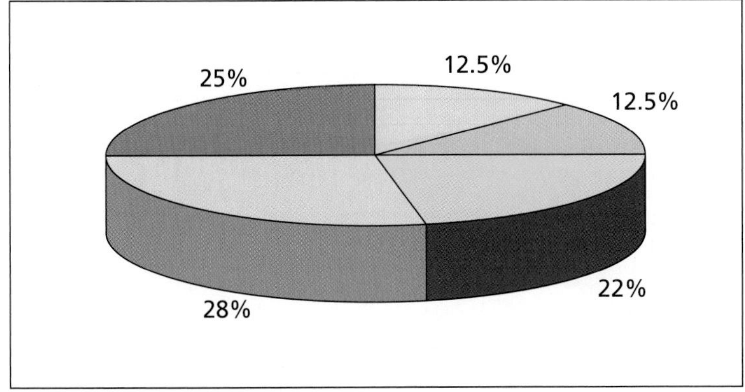

Figure 5-4 Example of a Pie Chart. Each section of this pie chart shows the percentage of various elements that make up the whole. Note that the visual size of each slice accurately represents the numbered percentages noted on the chart. This representation portrays a 3-D pie chart, but the same information could be represented in a simple two-dimensional chart.

5

- **Scatter charts** (sometimes called scatter plots) compare pairs of values under the same situations. A scatter chart is illustrated in Figure 5-5.

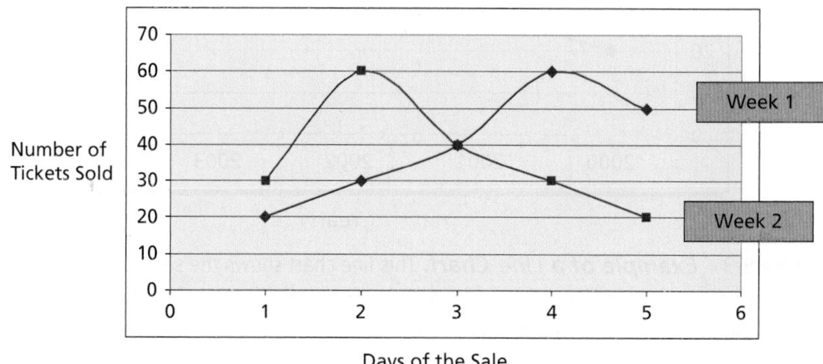

Figure 5-5 Example of a Scatter Chart. This scatter chart compares the number of tickets sold on each day of a two-week period. The lines have been added using Microsoft Excel.

5

- **Area charts** display trends and their magnitude over time, as illustrated in Figure 5-6. Area charts are similar to line charts, except that the area below the line is filled in. You can add 3-D effects, color, legends, labels, and animation to this type of chart, using Microsoft Excel.

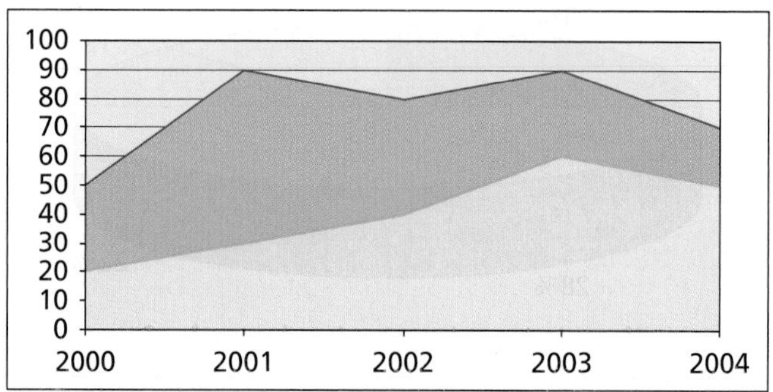

Figure 5-6 Example of an Area Chart. On this area chart, each filled area represents a value over time. The peak of each filled area represents the value (on the y-axis) of the categories represented on the x-axis.

PUT IT TO USE When using a graphic to present information, select the simplest graphic that communicates your message effectively. For various types of graphs, explore the types of graphs available in Microsoft Excel.

Graphics—illustrations, graphs, charts, photographs—must be appropriate to the content of your document or presentation and accurately convey the message you are sending. After you have determined where a graphic would be appropriate in your overall organizational plan, you must effectively organize the information represented in the graphic. Any documentation or sources for the data must be included in full. Several tips for working with commonly used graphics, some of which were described in the previous section of the text, are as follows (Minter, 2001):

- **Bar charts and line graphs.** These graphics are versatile, good for comparisons, and relatively easy to construct. In terms of recommendations, a title should be added directly above the chart or graph and horizontal (x) and vertical (y) axes should be labeled. Use as few bars or lines as possible and emphasize one aspect of the data by changing the color or texture of the bar or line.
- **Pie charts.** Your pie chart should include six or fewer slices with contrasting colors, shades of gray, or simple patterns to increase readability. Slices should be labeled and one piece of data can be emphasized by moving a slice out from the circle. As with bar charts and line graphs, a title should be placed above a pie chart.
- **Illustrations.** Diagrams, maps, and drawings are examples of illustrations. An illustration is used to convey a large amount of information in a small space. The rule of thumb is that if it needs a lot of explanation, it is probably too complicated for an illustration. Ample white space should be around and within the illustration and a title should be positioned above it.
- **Photographs.** Photographs can add a "human face" to data. Written permission should be obtained from subjects before their picture is used.

success steps for organizing graphics effectively

Organize graphics so:

- the reader can easily understand the graphic,
- the graphic elaborates on the information in the document or presentation,
- the image is selected for its ability to convey an accurate message,
- the table or chart or figure is able to stand alone,
- the table or chart or figure simplifies information,
- the graphic is as simple as possible,
- data are presented in relationship to a context, and
- pictures or cartoons illustrate ideas in the text.

ORGANIZING POWERPOINT PRESENTATIONS

Presentation software such as Microsoft PowerPoint offers opportunities to create impressive and fairly sophisticated presentations. When using presentation software, two levels of organization must be considered. First, the content must be arranged in a logical and understandable manner, using the concepts discussed earlier in this chapter. In addition, visual and spatial organization is important because the visual appeal of an electronic presentation has a significant impact on audience members and their response to the presentation.

The suggestions presented here are only general guidelines, and straying from the rules can increase the impact of your presentation at times. For example, pink, aqua, and bright yellow are typically not recommended as a good color combination for an entire PowerPoint presentation, but if you use these colors on one slide that refers to the pop culture of the 1980s, they can emphasize your message. Good judgment in considering your topic, audience, and other factors is always essential to creating effective presentations. Consider the following design recommendations for creating an effective PowerPoint presentation (College of Southern Nevada, 2011).

- **Select colors thoughtfully.** Color choice can have a significant effect on how viewers receive your presentation. For example, text that is difficult to read because of low contrast with the background may cause your viewers to "tune out" your presentation because it is too difficult to follow. Keep in mind the following points about color in your presentations.
  - Select color combinations that provide enough contrast to facilitate reading but are not so high contrast that they become distracting. Select colors that promote legibility.
  - Avoid colors that clash or form an unusual combination. Unorthodox color combinations can be effective if used sparingly and to support a specific theme but should not be used for an entire presentation.
  - Review Figure 5-7 for various examples of effective color choices.

Slide 1: Low-contrast colors are difficult to read.

Figure 5-7 Examples of Use of Color in PowerPoint. Effective PowerPoint slides should use basic colors with enough contrast for viewers to see the slide elements clearly. These examples show how color can be used on slides to advantage or disadvantage.

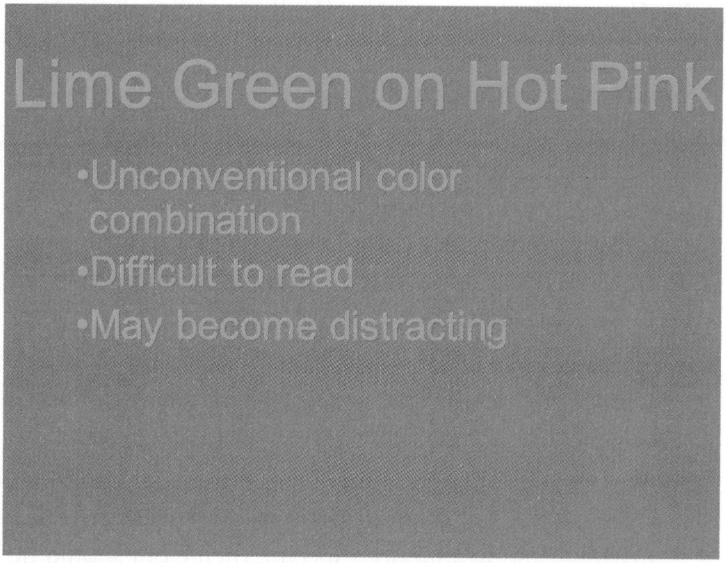

Slide 2: This color combination is unconventional and difficult to read.

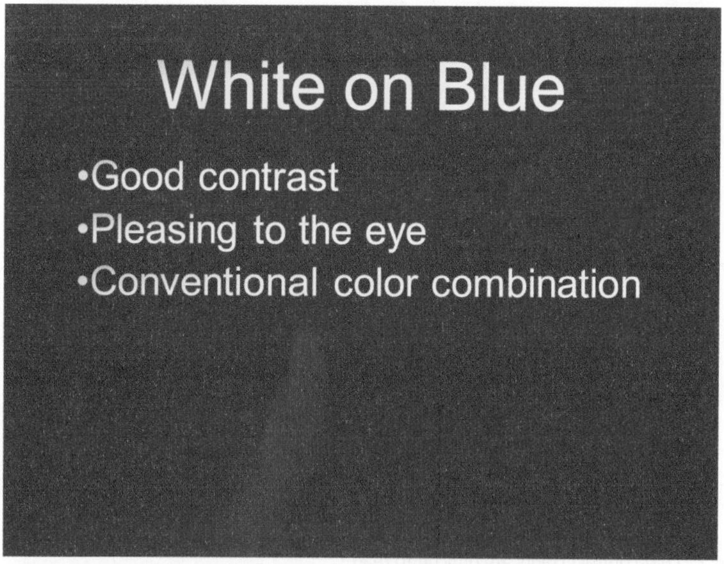

Slide 3: The conventional colors of blue and white are pleasing to the eye and are easily read.

Figure 5-7 *(Continued)*

- **Use legible fonts.** The text in a presentation must be legible to all members of the audience, yet not overwhelming. To maximize legibility, consider font size and style. Figure 5-8 provides examples.

Slide 1: Shows an embellished font that is difficult to read on the screen.

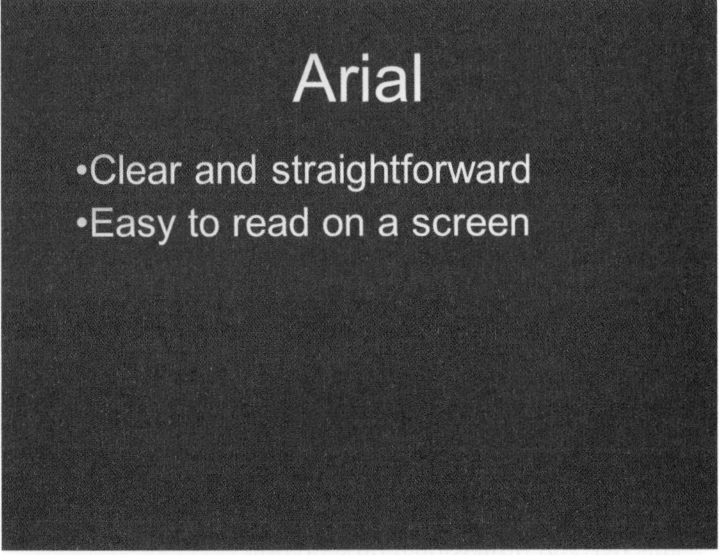

Slide 2: Shows a plain font that is easily read on the screen.

Figure 5-8 Examples of Fonts in PowerPoint. Compare Slide 1 with Slide 2, which are different fonts of the same size.

5

- The recommended font size is 44 for headings and 38 for bulleted points. Using a minimum font size of 28 is also recommended. Smaller font sizes become difficult to read, and larger font sizes may become overwhelming and be difficult to fit on the slide.
- Fonts should be of a standard and easy to read style, such as Arial, Tahoma, or Verdana. Intricate and embellished fonts are difficult to read on a screen.

- **Present information clearly and concisely.** Slides are only one part of the overall presentation. In addition, you will be explaining and possibly demonstrating the main points represented on the slides. Therefore, you should consider the slides as a supplement to guide viewers through the information you are presenting. To use the slides effectively, consider the following recommendations:
  - Set a limit of 5 lines per slide and 25 words per slide. Capture the main idea, and state it succinctly. Expand on each idea orally.
  - Use short bullets that emphasize or reinforce what you are discussing. Again, these are main ideas to guide the viewer. Your explanation will provide the details.
  - Use a larger font to state main ideas. PowerPoint automatically adjusts the font size as the levels of text decrease. Keeping that in mind, state the main idea on the higher levels of the PowerPoint outline and supporting ideas underneath. The main idea will be in larger font and the supporting ideas in smaller font.
  - Limit punctuation and avoid abbreviations that might be unclear to viewers.
  - Do not use all capitals or all lowercase letters. Use conventional grammar rules.

- **Create visual appeal.** The general organization and appearance of your presentation have an impact on your audience. The following are suggestions for creating an effective and professional presentation.
  - Select a plain or simple background that does not compete with your message. A solid color or a watermark background

that supports your theme is appropriate. Bold and busy backgrounds make the text difficult to read and detract from your message.

- Design charts that are simple, free from clutter, and contain a contrast of colors. These attributes make it easier for your audience to understand the information being conveyed in the chart.
- Avoid distracting slide transitions, text appearances, sounds, and multimedia content that plays automatically. If you do choose to use one of the custom features available in PowerPoint, select one that is subtle and that is consistent with the tone and message of your presentation.
- As with written documents, use graphics, such as pictures and clipart, only if they support the text and the theme of the presentation.

Critical Thinking Questions

- What is the best PowerPoint presentation you have seen? What made it effective?
- What is the worst PowerPoint presentation you have seen? Why was it ineffective?
- How can multimedia be used to increase the effectiveness of presentations? What types of multimedia would you consider when creating a presentation related to your field of study?

PUT IT TO USE Watch your PowerPoint presentation yourself before presenting to an audience. Evaluate it for legibility, clarity, and visual appeal. View the presentation from various perspectives to ensure that it is clearly visible from all vantage points. Verify that the length of the presentation is sufficient for the allotted time for discussing it.

PREZI: THE ZOOMING PRESENTATION EDITOR

Although PowerPoint is the most popular presentation software, there are alternatives that can make your presentations more distinct. One of these is Prezi, which you can access in a free and basic version at www.prezi.com. Unlike a PowerPoint presentation that contains many slides, a presentation on Prezi consists of one slide that contains all of your text and graphics. On that one slide you can focus your viewer's attention wherever you wish. You can move the focus of attention up, down, left, or right from topic to topic, called *panning*. Or you can also move the focus in and out from the topics and details, called *zooming*. Panning and zooming with Prezi can make your presentations stand out and be more effective, especially when the following suggestions are utilized.

- **Use panning to show relationships between topics.** Arrange your topics on the slide in a way that illustrates your point. For example, if you are telling a story or describing an event, you may wish to place your topics in a line from left to right to show their sequence. Or you may place them in a list from top to bottom to indicate importance.
- **Use grouping to avoid panning too much.** Quickly panning from one side of your presentation to the other can be distracting to your viewers, even disorienting. To avoid panning too much, place related topics fairly close to each other in groups.
- **Use zooming to show relationships between a topic and its supporting details.** PowerPoint presentations usually list the topic in the title and the details in bullets below on the same slide. Prezi allows you to focus first on the topic, zoom in to view the details, and then zoom in further to see more details if you wish.
- **Use layering to make zooming more effective.** When viewing a topic, make sure that the details are close to the topic, yet not quite big enough to be read. Zoom in to let your viewers read the details when you are ready. This technique, called *layering*, helps your viewers to focus first on the topic and then on the details while maintaining the connection between them.

OTHER PRESENTATION SOFTWARE

While PowerPoint is considered the standard bearer of presentation software and Prezi is continuing to grow, there is other software available with which you may come into contact (and therefore will need to become proficient at) in the workplace.

- **LibreOffice Impress.** Impress is presentation software that is part of the LibreOffice suite, which has functionality that is similar, if not comparable, to Microsoft Office. The suite, including the Impress application, is free and can be downloaded from https://www.libreoffice.org.
- **GoAnimate.** GoAnimate is a do-it-yourself animated video website. And while the product is not considered strictly

presentation software, it has significant business applications. One of the best features is that it allows the user to concentrate on the narrative, which can help in selling a product or a concept to others. There is an extensive content library where you can choose (and manipulate) characters, backgrounds, and other information to make a customized video in minutes. The finished product can then be downloaded, shared, or published on YouTube or Facebook.

- **Google Slides.** Google Slides is the free presentation app available to anyone with a Google account. Presentations can be customized with text, images, videos, or imported slides. Files created in Google Slides are stored on Google Drive, a cloud storage solution that allows the documents to be accessed from multiple computers or mobile devices and shared with others. This is especially helpful if you are working on a group project.
- **SlideSnack.** SlideSnack is an online presentation sharing tool that allows you to upload a presentation (such as PowerPoint, Keynote, or Word) as a .pdf file. From there you can create a *slidecast,* which is presentation plus voice. The presentation can then be shared over any social media site or downloaded as video and distributed over YouTube, Vimeo, or other video sharing service (Hung, 2013).

SELF-ASSESSMENT QUESTIONS

- How proficient do you think you are at using PowerPoint?
- What features do you think might make Prezi the more desirable presentation software to use?
- What other uses might you find for Google Drive?

5

APPLICATION AND USES OF ORGANIZED INFORMATION

Organized information has several standard uses in the professional world. Proposals, grants, and technical reports are documents that are common to many fields. Each has a well-established format and uses information in specific ways. Understanding how each report or document uses various types of information will maximize your effectiveness in preparing or reviewing these documents. You may encounter other types and applications of information in the workplace. Proposals, grants, and technical reports are covered here.

PUT IT TO USE Parts of the following formats for professional papers also can apply to assignments that you complete in school. Although there is no standard structure for school assignments, relevant parts of the following report formats can be incorporated into your assignments based on your instructor's requirements. Select those that support your assignment goals, and use them as your guidelines.

PROPOSALS AND GRANTS

Proposals are usually written to suggest a program or an action. Grants are written to obtain funding for research or a project. Proposals and grants are covered together here, as their organization and the information they contain are similar. Specific elements of a grant or proposal will vary depending on the situation. The components used as an example here are based on guidelines from the *Catalog of Federal Domestic Assistance* (n.d.).

5

- **Summary.** The summary of a proposal is normally brief (several paragraphs) and provides an overview of the proposed project. Because a summary is the first page of a proposal, it makes the first impression. Therefore, effective organization of information and presentation of the primary objectives of the project are critical.
- **Introduction.** The Introduction in a proposal is its foundation and plays a significant role in establishing your credibility. The introduction provides general information about participants in the project, the organization, organizational goals, and a history of their activities. Use Bloom's *knowledge* level to organize the introduction.
- **Statement of problem and purpose.** This statement clearly describes the problem or issue being addressed, as well as the benefits the program will provide. Other issues that are addressed in this section include a brief history of the problem, current programs that address it, and how the proposal supplements these programs. Also important is to present alternatives for continuing the program when current funding

is depleted. Bloom's stage of *analysis* and critical thinking skills are applied in this phase.

- **Objectives.** The Objectives portion states what the project is intended to achieve and the methods that will be used to meet the goals. Goals must be measurable and realistic, and the project will be evaluated based on how effectively the stated goals are met. Creating feasible and meaningful goals requires the synthesis of needs, reality, and creative thinking and ideas.
- **Action plan.** The Action Plan in the proposal relies heavily on Bloom's level of *synthesis*. This plan outlines the sequence of activities that will lead to achievement of the goals. Graphics such as a flowchart or a table can be used to effectively explain the sequence of project events.
- **Evaluation.** The Evaluation phase of a project covers evaluation of the final product as well as the process leading to it. Projects are commonly evaluated on how well they met the objectives and goals, how closely the plans were followed, and how the project met the needs stated at the beginning of the project. Bloom's *evaluation* stage is a way to think about organizing information for this last stage of a proposal.

TECHNICAL REPORTS

Technical reports are common in the workplace, to communicate the results of a project or research. Technical reports typically contain the following elements and are organized accordingly (Sherman, 1996), with some variation, depending on your situation.

- **Title.** The title should be concise, yet describe the content of the report.
- **Author information.** The author's name, title, professional affiliation, and contact information should be provided.
- **Abstract.** The abstract is a brief yet thorough overview of the report's contents. The abstract summarizes the findings and results and can be used as a concise version of the entire paper. Writing an effective abstract requires strong analysis and synthesis skills.

- **Keywords.** The keywords provide parameters of the report and may be used to search for additional information on the topic.
- **Body of the report.** The body of the report contains all the relevant material. Depending on the type of information, the written body of the report can be organized in a variety of ways, as described in this chapter. For example, a research project might be sequenced chronologically. The body of the report requires skills related to Bloom's levels of *application*, *analysis*, and *synthesis* as you explain what you did, your findings, your interpretations, and explanation of new ideas that emerge from your work.
- **Acknowledgments.** Here, you recognize and express appreciation to individuals who helped or supported you in your project.
- **References.** The sources referred to are documented according to the guidelines in the recommended style book.
- **Appendices.** Documents that support your report but did not flow with the body of the report are included as appendices. Appendices should be referenced in the text according to your style book.

5

PUT IT TO USE If you are required to develop a specialized report, follow the guidelines provided to you. Additional information may be found online by conducting a search using the type of report you are doing as the keyword.

CHAPTER SUMMARY

In this chapter, you learned the importance of organizing information that conveys your message effectively to your specific audience. To do so, you learned that it must be prepared effectively, using methods such as alphabetical, hierarchical, or others. The method selected depends on the type of information. In addition, the presentation format must be appropriate for the audience and type of information and may include visual organizers, various types of reports, or other formats.

POINTS TO KEEP IN MIND

- Effective organization of information is a critical part of information literacy.
- Effective organization of information, both in the preparation and presentation phases, is essential to your credibility.
- Information should be organized and presented according to its type, your goal, and the intended audience.

apply it

Activity #1: Creating a Visual Organizer

GOAL: To create and use a visual organizer to organize information.

STEP 1: Select a topic for which you would like to organize information. The topic should be fairly complex, and you should have a genuine need to organize the information related to the topic.

STEP 2: Research visual organizers on the Internet. Suggested search terms are "visual organizers" and "concept maps."

STEP 3: Select a visual organizer that suits your needs and learning style. Use it to organize the information related to your topic. You may want to try several organizers to see which is most helpful to you.

Activity #2: Selecting the Best Way to Present Data

GOAL: To select the most effective presentation methods for various types of information.

STEP 1: Distribute three small index cards to each group member. Ask each group member to record one type of data on each of the cards. The data should be representative of an aspect of your field.

STEP 2: Randomly select from the completed cards. As a group, decide which graphic would best convey the information. Support your choice with a rationale.

STEP 3: Create the graphic you have chosen. Make sure that it meets the criteria for an effective graphic. Decide on the type of graphic, color choice, added effects, labels and legends, and so forth. Explain how your choices enhance the presentation of the information.

STEP 4: Complete as many versions of steps 2 and 3 as possible.

continued

continued

Activity #3: Creating a PowerPoint Presentation

GOAL: To apply suggested practices for creating an effective PowerPoint presentation.

STEP 1: Select a topic that is of interest to you and that you would like to present in PowerPoint.

STEP 2: Create a PowerPoint presentation on your topic according to the guidelines recommended in this chapter. Seek additional information if needed.

STEP 3: Present your PowerPoint slides to an audience. Ask viewers to give a constructive critique of your work.

Activity #4: Webpage Exploration

GOAL: To develop an awareness of effective webpage design and organization.

STEP 1: Review as many webpages as possible related to a topic of interest.

STEP 2: Evaluate each website according to the criteria listed in the chapter. Print the page, and record your observations directly on the page.

STEP 3: Review your observations and determine which sites were appealing and why. Compile a reference of webpage design tips and ideas that you can use in the future.

5

SUGGESTED ITEMS FOR LEARNING PORTFOLIO

Refer to the "How to Use This Book" section at the beginning of this textbook for more information on learning portfolios.

- Webpage design tips and ideas

REFERENCES

Catalog of Federal Domestic Assistance. (n.d.). *Developing and Writing a Grant Proposal.* Retrieved June 17, 2013, from https://www.cfda.gov/?static=grants&s=generalinfo&mode=list&tab=list&tabmode=list

Huitt, W. (2003). The information processing approach to cognition. *Educational Psychology Interactive.* Valdosta, GA: Valdosta State University. Retrieved June 17, 2013, from http://www.edpsycinteractive.org/topics/cognition/infoproc.html

Hung, A. (2013). *The 6 Best Business Presentation Software Alternatives to PowerPoint.* Retrieved June 17, 2013, from http://goanimate.com/video-maker-tips/6-best-business-presentation-software-and-powerpoint-alternatives/

Minter, E. (2001). *Using Graphics to Report Evaluation Data.* Retrieved February 5, 2016, from http://learningstore.uwex.edu/Assets/pdfs/G3658-13.pdf

College of Southern Nevada - Center for Academic & Professional Excellence (2011). *Tips for Effective PowerPoint Presentations.* Retrieved March 11, 2016, from http://sites.csn.edu/cape/documents/Tips%20for%20Effective%20PowerPoint%20Presentations.pdf

Sherman, A. (1996). *Some Advice on Writing a Technical Report.* Retrieved June 17, 2013, from http://www.csee.umbc.edu/~sherman/Courses/documents/TR_how_to.html

Stucker, C. (2006). *Organizing Information the Way People Use It.* EzineArticles.com. Retrieved June 17, 2013, from http://ezinearticles.com/?Organizing-Information-the-Way-People-Use-It&id=113311

Wurman, R. S. (2000). LATCH: *The Five Ultimate Hatracks.* Retrieved June 17, 2013, from http://www.informit.com/articles/article.aspx?p=130881&seqNum=6

CHAPTER OUTLINE

Solving Information Problems: Communicate the Information
Intellectual Property
Copyright
Plagiarism
Citing Information Sources
Information and Privacy Issues
Information and Security Issues
The Importance of Information Literacy in the Workplace

SelectStock/the Agency Collection/Getty Images

Legal and Ethical Issues Related to Information

LEARNING OBJECTIVES

By the end of this chapter, you will be able to:

- Explain how privacy and security can be breached and protected in both print and electronic environments.
- Define and describe intellectual property, copyright, and fair use of copyrighted material and how they relate to using information legally and ethically.
- Define plagiarism and discuss ways to avoid plagiarizing another's work.
- Explain how to cite various information sources.
- Describe the importance of information literacy in the workplace.

BE IN THE KNOW

Teamwork

You may have heard the expression "There is no *I* in team." While this statement is both literally and figuratively true, there are several "I" statements of which you should be aware as they pertain to being a successful team member in both the classroom and the workplace. As you will read later on in this chapter, employers place high value on an employee's ability to be a fully participative member of a team and the importance of and its relationship to information literacy.

Consider the following points. Read them and put yourself in a team situation. Do you agree with these statements as they apply to you? What actions might you take to make yourself a better team member?

- *I* need to be accountable to my team members to complete the work I have been assigned.
- *I* am as valued as a team member as anyone else on the team.
- *I* value the contributions of all team members.
- *I* fully participate in discussions and decisions that affect the outcome of the project.
- *I* am a team leader and other team members look to me to fill that role.
- *I* weigh all suggestions equally before coming to a conclusion.
- *I* care about the success of the project as much for my team members as I do for myself.
- *I* meet or exceed deadlines and provide quality work that positively affects the outcome of the project.
- *I* voice my opinions and concerns to the team in order to make the project as successful as possible.
- *I* recognize that different team members bring different skills to the team.

What other "I" statements can you think of as they relate to being a successful team member? GO TEAM!

6

SOLVING INFORMATION PROBLEMS: COMMUNICATE THE INFORMATION

As we have discussed so far, an information-literate individual knows how to define the need for research, find the information in the library or on the Internet, evaluate the information, and organize the information. The last critical component of information literacy is the ability to use information legally and ethically and communicate it effectively to others—Step 5 in the research process, as shown in Figure 6-1.

Legal and ethical aspects of information include the concepts of intellectual property, copyright, plagiarism, and fair use. Additional

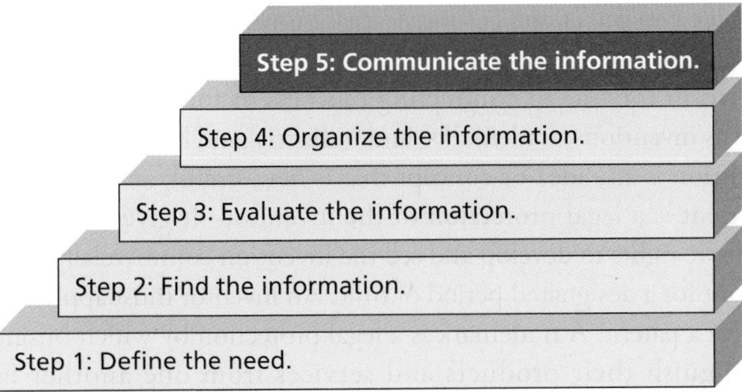

Figure 6-1 Research Process Step 5. Communicate the Information. The last step of a research project should be to effectively communicate the information.

legal and ethical considerations involve privacy and security issues when communicating information as well as how the Fourth Amendment of the Constitution impacts the search and seizure of mobile phones. In regards to the latter, the Supreme Court unanimously ruled in June 2014 that police would be required to obtain a warrant to search cell phones (Mears, 2014).

This chapter addresses these aspects of communicating the information found during the research process. It is not meant to provide legal counsel or advice but is intended only to discuss the types of issues that you, as an information-literate professional, should consider.

INTELLECTUAL PROPERTY

Intellectual property refers to anything created by the mind, such as literary works (books, poems, essays), artwork (drawings, paintings), inventions, ideas, logos or symbols, names, designs, images or photographs, and other types of multimedia (animation, interactive content). In general, the concept of intellectual property treats anything created by the mind (or intellect) the same as any material property and gives owners of intellectual property rights similar to those of material property owners. When conducting research and using information, then, the intellectual property of others, or things others have thought of, must be respected. Likewise, if you create something, your own creation becomes your intellectual property that others must respect.

The two major areas of intellectual property are industrial property and copyright. Industrial property refers to intellectual property created in the line of conducting business or for business purposes, such as inventions, trademarks, and industrial and business designs. An invention is any idea or concept that is new, useful, and not obvious. A patent is a legal protection of the invention. It gives the inventor exclusive rights to develop and sell the invention commercially to make a profit for a designated period of time. An inventor must apply for and receive a patent. A trademark is a legal protection by which businesses distinguish their products and services from one another using identifying elements such as logos, names, and symbols. Trademark holders retain the rights to use their protected elements exclusively during the operation of their business. Industrial design rights protect the aesthetics or appearance, design, or style of the originator.

Copyright protects other forms of intellectual property, such as literary works, artwork, music, audio and video productions, photographs, and newspaper articles. All of these protections of intellectual property can be bought, sold, and transferred or licensed to third parties. The purpose of intellectual-property protection laws is to encourage creation and innovation for the public good by protecting the producing individuals, businesses, and organizations from exploitation. Other types of intellectual property apply to specific purposes, such as materials related to geographical indication, personality rights, plant breeders' rights, trade secrets, and others. Most relevant to the discussion in this chapter is copyright and its implications in the use and communication of information.

Self-Assessment Questions

- What intellectual property have you created yourself that you would not like others to use without your permission?
- How would you respond if other people were to present your intellectual creations as their own? Write down your feelings.

COPYRIGHT

Copyright reflects the rights given to creators of some forms of expressions of intellectual property, such as literary and artistic works. Copyrights are protected by copyright laws. Ideas are not copyrighted; only the expression of those ideas in some documented format can be copyrighted. Ideas in the form of procedures, methods, facts, techniques, styles, and mathematical concepts cannot be copyrighted. Figure 6-2 provides examples of expressions covered by copyright law.

▪ Novels	▪ Films
▪ Poems	▪ Paintings
▪ Plays	▪ Drawings
▪ Reference works	▪ Photographs
▪ Articles in periodicals	▪ Sculptures
▪ Computer programs	▪ Architecture
▪ Databases	▪ Advertisements
▪ Musical compositions	▪ Maps
▪ Choreography	▪ Technical drawings
▪ Applets	▪ Songs
▪ Web pages	▪ Images

Figure 6-2 Examples of Copyrighted Materials.

The goal of a copyright is to protect the original creators of the work (and their heirs). Copyright assures that the original creator of the work can do with the work whatever he or she wants. The original creators have the right to authorize someone else to use the work, prohibit others from using their work, or sell their copyright to someone else. This means that they can give up their rights (usually for a negotiated fee) to someone else, who then becomes the copyright owner. This new owner becomes protected by copyright law, as was the original owner.

Copyright law was founded in the Intellectual Property Clause of the U.S. Constitution, initially enacted as the Copyright Act of 1790 (Patry, 1994, 2000). The Copyright Act of 1976 is the basis of current copyright law (United States Code, 2014). Advances in technology and the Internet result in the law being revised continually to reflect current needs and issues. The information-literate professional stays updated on changes in the law that affects the use of information.

Copyright law regulates more than just "copying" the work. It also controls translating the material into another language, performing the material (as in a play), copying electronic versions of a work (as in music or movies on CD, DVD, or Blu-ray), and broadcasting copyrighted material (on radio, TV, or over the Internet). In short, copyright covers reproducing a work in any way. Copyright laws protect creators of original works by assuring that they receive their due recognition and economic rewards associated with their creation.

Once an individual or a group creates an original work, this work is considered to be copyrighted simply by its existence. Although

6

copyright is not dependent upon registration, creators of original material can document their ownership by registering a work with the United States Copyright Office. Registration using paper forms involves a processing time of up to 13 months. Alternatively, the process can be completed within eight months using the U.S. Copyright Office's eCO Registration System to e-file (United States Copyright Office, 2016). The copyright symbol © is used to identify a copyrighted work. Copyright protection is documented, for a fee, to the originator of the expression for a specified time limit, such as life of the originator plus several years to allow the originator's heirs to benefit from the copyrighted work (University System of Georgia Board of Regents, n.d. [a]). Documenting a copyright protects the owner of the work by allowing him or her to sue another individual who uses the work without appropriate permission. The exact copyright terms can be complicated and depend on several factors, including when the work was published and created.

When a copyright expires, the work is transferred into the public domain. The time after which a copyright expires depends on the type of work, its publication date, and other factors. When the work moves to the public domain, it no longer is protected by copyright and anyone can use it. Information-literate individuals ensure that they do not have to obtain permission to use originally copyrighted materials by checking with the United States Copyright Office to get a specific copyright expiration date for the material in question. And regardless of copyright status, it is courteous and professional to credit the original creator (University System of Georgia Board of Regents, n.d. [b]).

Fair use means that in some cases you can copy and distribute copyrighted materials without permission from or payment to the copyright holder. In general, fair use allows some limited copyrighted materials for educational, research, and other purposes. Fair-use laws are complicated and not defined clearly. Information-literate individuals seek clarification of the law when they are uncertain.

PLAGIARISM

Using someone else's original work without acknowledging the original creator is termed plagiarism. The work can be an idea, actual language, or some other original material. Plagiarism is a growing problem in educational and professional settings, and information-literate individuals take care to avoid this unethical and illegal practice.

Examples of plagiarism are:

- copying another person's work and submitting it as your own.
- presenting work completed by someone else as your own.
- taking an idea from someone else and submitting it as your own.
- copying text into an original document without indicating the text with quotation marks or correctly acknowledging the original creator of the work.
- paraphrasing someone else's work too closely and submitting it as your own.
- writing down words spoken by someone else in a face-to-face, telephone, or electronic discussion and submitting them as your own without acknowledging the original source.
- copying diagrams, photographs, images, charts, tables, clip art, and similar infographics as your own without obtaining permission and giving proper credit.
- reusing any media that is in electronic form, such as audio files, video files, applets, and software programs, without obtaining permission and giving proper credit to the original creator.
- submitting an assignment that has been purchased through a paper mill or other custom writing service.

Regardless of the type of material, if the work of others is presented without giving them proper credit or citing the source of the work properly, this constitutes plagiarism.

You do not have to document anything that is your original creation or idea. Examples of things you do not have to document are:

- your own experiences, observations, insights, thoughts, and conclusions.
- your own results from personal observation of an experiment or study.
- your own artistic or literary creations such as prose, poems, diagrams, artwork, audio recordings, video recordings, and photographs.

- facts that are generally accepted as being true.
- common knowledge or observations considered to be common sense.
- historical events, myths, and legends.

STRATEGIES FOR AVOIDING PLAGIARISM

To avoid plagiarizing someone else's information, several strategies are outlined as follows:

- **Quote.** Using another's exact words is acceptable, but you must copy the exact words, use quotation marks around the quoted words, and cite the source properly. Quotation marks should be used whether the copied words are spoken or written. When adding your own words to quoted text, you must put your words in brackets to distinguish them from the quoted material. Adding your own words is necessary sometimes to put the quote in context or to fill in missing words so the entire message can be understood more easily.
- **Paraphrase.** Paraphrasing means rephrasing the words of someone else. It is acceptable as long as the meaning is not changed and the originator is credited properly with a citation. Paraphrasing involves more than rearranging the order of words or changing minor elements of a passage. Read the original material and, without looking at it, rewrite the content using your own words. If you have to intersperse exact phrases from the original, place these words within quotation marks. The paraphrase is followed by a statement giving credit to the original author. An example of a paraphrase is as follows:

  > According to Smith, when children eat too much sugar, they display abnormal behavior for several minutes and then show significant signs of fatigue and irritation.

- **Summarize.** Summarizing requires condensing a significant amount of someone else's work into a shorter statement or paragraph. As is the case with paraphrasing, this is acceptable as long as the meaning is not changed and the originator is given proper credit with a citation. To accomplish this, read the original information and then try to condense the content without looking. If you have used any exact text, place it within quotation marks. Also, place quotation marks around any special words taken from the original text.

- **Take effective notes.** To reduce the likelihood of plagiarism, it is a good idea to take careful notes so you can remember exactly which ideas are yours and which are someone else's ideas. One way to keep track is to develop a note-taking strategy that includes a notation or symbol for your idea (such as *MINE*) and a notation or symbol for the ideas of the author of the work (such as *AU*). If notes are being typed into a word processing program, such as Microsoft Word, the comment feature can also be used as part of your note-taking strategy. Put all direct quotes in quotation marks. When you take notes, designate *AU* next to facts, quotes (with quotation marks), paraphrased sentences, and summaries of the author's work. When you write down your own insights and thoughts, use *MINE* (or whatever designation you choose). And be sure to clearly label the source of the information on each page of your notes.
- **Save your work.** You can take several measures to maintain the security of your own work. To prevent others from plagiarizing your work, keep copies of your draft work in separate files. For example, rather than revising your original file, save the first draft as draft 1, your second draft as draft 2, and so forth. This will be a reminder that you actually did the work yourself. Save copies of your files in separate places, and make at least one hard copy of your work. Do not allow others to access your computer files.

You can further protect your computer and original work by saving documents as protected files that require a password for access. Use the search feature on the "Help" menu of the software you are using to learn the steps for creating a password to protect your documents. Of course, you will have to remember the password so you can open your file. This procedure works in most Microsoft Office applications. Other applications have similar features. If you plan on distributing a document to other people, consider saving it as an Adobe PDF file that can be read, but not edited.

- **Use plagiarism detection software.** The advent of the Internet has made plagiarism easier than ever. Cyber plagiarism, as it is known, has seen a dramatic rise in recent years, especially by students and content writers (bloggers, writers, and other professionals). Schools, colleges, and universities now routinely check for plagiarism using plagiarism-detection software, such as Turnitin. In addition, identifying content plagiarized from websites can often be accomplished by searching for the first line of the material in a web browser. You can also avoid a costly mistake by using free software, such as Dupli Checker (http://duplichecker.com) to detect any plagiarism in your work. An information-literate person knows that unintentional plagiarism is still plagiarism.
- **Manage your time.** Schedule the periods of time in which you intend to study and complete your assignments. This practice is helpful in ensuring you will be effective and efficient in your planning, researching, and writing. As part of this process, it is important that time be allocated to carefully review your work and verify that all sources have been properly cited.
- **Read and rewrite.** An effective way to avoid plagiarizing is to read the original source, put it away, and complete your writing based on your reading. When your writing is complete, return to the original work and check your facts for accuracy. Cite references appropriately.
- **Apply the information.** Discuss the information you are using in the context of your assignment. Expand on ideas. Apply the information in a unique way to the topic at hand. Refer to the original thought or fact, but apply it creatively to your project using your own original ideas.
- **Cite your sources appropriately.** Sources should be referenced in the text as well as in the reference list. There are several acceptable styles of source citation and reference, and you should follow the style prescribed by your instructor.

In addition to upholding your own responsibility for being honest, it is important to participate in helping to make your learning environment one of high integrity. Honest students need to report any possible cheating and plagiarism that may be occurring.

Personally confronting a classmate may or may not be an option, but reporting the episode is critical so that the situation can be properly addressed.

PUT IT TO USE There should be no difference when considering the intellectual property rights for electronic sources and other resources. The same consideration should be given to intellectual property found on the Internet as with any other information source.

POTENTIAL CONSEQUENCES OF PLAGIARIZING

Plagiarizing another's work and getting caught for doing so comes with dire consequences. If you are in the workforce, the chances of getting fired, or at least being formally warned and written up in your personnel file, are very real.

Being accused of plagiarizing while in school is no less consequential. All institutions of higher learning regard cheating and plagiarism very seriously. Academic policies and procedures clearly spell out rules about academic honesty and integrity, and schools place this information in college catalogs and online on the school's website or portal.

Oftentimes course syllabi will address the school's use of Turnitin or other plagiarism detection software as a standard operating procedure. As reading and adhering to syllabi is a course requirement, the mention of the use of such software by the institution puts you on further notice that plagiarism will not be tolerated.

The information-literate person recognizes what constitutes plagiarism and the resulting penalties that follow. Be sure you are that person.

CITING INFORMATION SOURCES

As discussed, to avoid plagiarism and infringement on someone else's intellectual property, you will have to properly cite and document the sources of information in your materials. Even if you do not quote or paraphrase the source directly, if the source contributed significantly to your document, you should cite it properly. In addition to crediting the author appropriately, proper citation allows the reader to go to your sources to verify facts or obtain additional information. It also shows that you actually conducted sound research rather than randomly providing or fabricating information.

There are many acceptable ways to cite information sources. Methods for writing citations and reference lists are available in writing style guides. These guides prescribe exact formats for writing, punctuating, referencing sources within text, and citing sources in reference areas. Many professions, businesses, and academic institutions prefer or require use of one style over another, and some publishers specify the style you are to use. You should become familiar with the style and follow it consistently. In addition, newly published editions of style guides should be reviewed so you are aware of any recent changes that may have occurred.

Common style guides and examples of citations according to each are outlined next. Each of these guides specifies exactly how various types of citations are to be structured, including punctuation and use of italics, and how the elements are ordered. The guides provide specific styles for many types of resources, such as books, chapters in books, journals, articles in journals, magazines and magazine articles. Additional examples include newspapers and newspaper articles, review articles, online resources, and websites.

APA STYLE

The *Publication Manual of the American Psychological Association* (www.apastyle.org) is the style prescribed by the American Psychological Association (APA). This style typically is used in the fields of psychology, health, and social sciences:

Publication Manual of the American Psychological Association, 6th ed. (2010). Washington, DC: American Psychological Association.

Correct APA style for citation of a book, e-book, or chapters with one author:

Author's Last Name, First Initial. Middle Initial. (Year). *Title of book with one author: Subtitle of book*. Location of publisher: Publisher.

Correct APA style for citation of an article of a journal:

Author's Last Name, First Initial. Middle Initial. (Year). Title of article within the journal. *Title of Journal, Volume number*, page number range.

Correct APA style for citation of a webpage:

Author's Last Name, First Initial. Middle Initial. (Year, Month Day). *Title of document.* Retrieved Month day, year, from http://web address (Note: No punctuation follows the web address, to ensure accuracy in retrieving.)

Correct APA style for citation of a video:

Producer's Last Name, First Initial. Middle Initial. (Producer). (Year). *Title of video* [Mode]. Country of origin: Studio.

Correct APA style for citation of an online video:

Producer's Last Name, First Initial. Middle Initial. (Year). *Title of video* [Mode]. Available Date of access, from complete URL

Correct APA style for citation of motion pictures:

Producer's Last Name, First Initial. Middle Initial. (Producer), & Director's Last Name, First Initial. Middle Initial. (Director). (Year). *Title of motion picture* [Motion picture]. Country of origin: Studio.

Correct APA style for citation of music recordings:

Writer's Last Name, First Initial. Middle Initial. (Copyright year). Title of song [Recorded by B. B. Artist if different from writer]. On *Title of album* [Medium of recording: CD, record, cassette, etc.] Location: Label. (Date of recording if different from song copyright date).

Correct APA style for citation of photographs:

Photographer's Last Name, First Initial. Middle Initial. (Date of composition (if unknown use n.d.)). *Title of work.* Museum or collection, City of collection or museum. Retrieved from Name of database.

Correct APA style for citation of online photographs:

Photographer's Last Name, First Initial. Middle Initial. (Date of composition (if unknown use n.d.)). *Title of work*. Museum or collection, City of collection or museum. Retrieved Date of access, from complete URL of website.

Correct APA style for citation of archived personal communication (i.e., oral histories):

Last Name, First Initial. Middle Initial. of person interviewed. (Date of Interview). Interview by First initial. Middle initial. Last Name [mode of medium]. Project title, Project sponsor. Location of archive, city.

Correct APA style for citation of magazines:

Author's Last Name, First Initial. Middle Initial. (Date of Publication). Title of article. *Name of Magazine*, volume, pages.

Correct APA style for citation of magazines from electronic sources:

6

Author's Last Name, First Initial. Middle Initial. (Date of Publication). Title of article. *Name of Magazine*, volume, pages. (If retrieved from a Database, then citation should look like a print citation.)

Author's Last Name, First Initial. Middle Initial. (Date of Publication). Title of article. *Name of Magazine*, volume, pages. Retrieved from complete URL.

Correct APA style for citation of newspapers:

Author's Last Name, First Initial. Middle Initial. (Date of Publication). Article title. *Newspaper Title*, edition, section, pages (p./pp.).

Correct APA style for citation of online newspapers:

Author's Last Name, First Initial. Middle Initial. (Date of Publication). Article title. *Newspaper Title*. Retrieved from complete URL.

MLA STYLE

The *MLA Style Manual and Guide to Scholarly Publishing* is the style guide of the Modern Language Association of America (MLA) (www.mla.org). This style typically is used in the fields of arts, literature, and humanities.

MLA Handbook. 8th ed. New York: Modern Language Association of America, 2016.

MLA style uses a group of core elements when citing sources. An element should be omitted if it isn't relevant to the source. Each of these core elements is listed and described as follows per the *MLA Handbook*:

1. **Author.** The first element in an MLA citation is the author, beginning with his or her last name, followed by a comma, the rest of the name, and ending with a period. For example, "Frost, Robert." When there are two authors, include both in the order they appear in the text. If there are three or more authors, include the first author, followed by et al. For example, "Frost, Robert, et al."
2. **Title of source.** After the author, the next element that you should include is the title of the source followed by a period. If the source is part of a larger text, such as a poem in an anthology, put the title in quotation marks. If the source is not part of a larger text, italicize the title.
3. **Title of container.** A container is the larger text that your source is part of. You should typically put the container title in italics, followed by a comma. Examples of containers include periodicals, websites, and television shows.
4. **Other contributors.** There may be people, in addition to authors, whose names are credited in a source, such as editors and contributors. You should include these additional names when their participation is important to your research or to the identification of the source. Include the description of a contributor, followed by his or her name.
5. **Version.** A source may be identified as a version when it is released in more than one form. A common version is an edition of books. If the source is a version of a work, include

that in your citation. Follow the version with a comma. Examples include "7th ed.," and "unabridged version,"

6. **Number.** In some cases, the source you are citing may be part of a numbered series of books, such as an encyclopedia or journal. Include the number of the source you are using.
7. **Publisher.** The publisher is responsible for producing the source or making it available to the public, and is typically an organization. You can often find the publisher on a title page or copyright page of a book or website.
8. **Publication date.** It is important to include the date of publication for your source when it is available. If you find more than one date, such as for a newspaper article in print versus a newspaper article online, include the date that is most meaningful or relevant to your purpose.
9. **Location.** The location will vary depending on the medium of the source that you choose. The location in a printed source will likely be the page or pages that the content appears on. An online source's location may be the URL or the digital object identifier (DOI).

MLA style also has a number of optional elements, in addition to the nine core elements, including adding the date of access for an online source that can be changed or removed at any time. For a complete list of the optional elements, search online or in the handbook.

While the core elements stay the same, your citations may include a variety of these pieces depending on what information is available for your source. You can use MLA citation rules for many source types, and several of the most commonly used are as follows:

Correct MLA style for citation of a book with an author's name:

Author's Last Name, Author's First Name. *Title of source*. Publisher, publication date.

Correct MLA style for citation of a book without an author's name:

Organization. *Title of source*. Publisher, publication date.

Correct MLA style for citation of an article of a periodical (journal, magazine, newspaper):

Author's Last Name, Author's First Name. "Title of article." Title of the Periodical, Volume, issue, year, page number range.

Correct MLA style for citation of a website:

Author's Last Name, Author's First Name. *Title of website.* Day Month Year of access, http://webpage address

Correct MLA style for citation of an article at a website:

Author's Last Name, Author's First Name. "Title: Subtitle of webpage." *Title of website.* Day Month Year of access, http://webpage address

CHICAGO STYLE

The Chicago Manual of Style (www.chicagomanualofstyle.org) is published by the University of Chicago Press. This style guide has the widest use overall, including the fields of history and other humanities. The official publication is:

The Chicago Manual of Style. 16th ed. 2010. Chicago: University of Chicago Press.

6

Correct Chicago style for citation of a book with one author:

Author's Last Name, First Name Middle Name/Initial. Date. *Title of Book with One Author: Subtitle of Book.* Location of publisher: Publisher.

Correct Chicago style for citation of an article of a journal:

Author's Last Name, First Name Middle Name/Initial. "Title of Article." *Title of Journal,* Volume no. (year): page number range.

Correct Chicago style for citation of a webpage:

Author's Last Name, First Name Middle Name/Inital. "Title of webpage." Location: sponsor, n.d. (means no date on the webpage) http://web address (accessed Month day, year).

Correct Chicago style for citation of film, television, and other recorded mediums:

First Name Last Name, *Title of Work*, Format, directed/performed by First Name Last Name (Original release year; City: Studio/Distributor, Video release year.), Medium.

You can learn more about citing sources by checking these style guides online or in the reference section of your local library. There are many additional digital resources that discuss citations and style guides as well. Conduct a search for Purdue Online Writing Lab and see what else you can learn about citations.

Critical Thinking Questions

- What citation style is used or required at your learning institution?
- What style is usually recommended for works related to your field of study?

PUT IT TO USE See the respective style manuals for correct citations of other types of information sources. Check for free downloads or PDFs of style manuals as well.

INFORMATION AND PRIVACY ISSUES

6

For the general public, privacy means keeping private information out of public view or access. For celebrities and otherwise famous (or infamous) people, privacy means keeping their personal lives out of public view. Enormous controversy abounds over privacy today, especially when national security is involved. Do the privacy rights of individuals supersede the collective rights of the general public to be safe? Or is it the other way around?

Privacy and information literacy means that individuals should maintain the privacy of other individuals' personal information. For example, the Health Insurance Portability and Accountability Act (HIPAA) of 1996 protects your medical information in a variety of ways. The actual act and extensive information concerning its implementation can be found at the Health and Human Services website (www.hhs.gov). Similarly, other types of privileged information, such as legal information, are protected by laws.

The Privacy Act of 1974 also provides many rights to U.S. citizens. For more information, see the U.S. Department of Justice website (www.usdoj.gov).

Although it is not part of U.S. law, a landmark "right to be forgotten" law was passed by the European Court of Justice in 2014 allowing Europeans to make requests to search engines, such as Google, to remove online content they feel misrepresents them and is no longer relevant. The decision was well received by privacy advocates but admonished by advocates of free speech (Manjoo, 2015).

Privacy rights are becoming increasingly important because the Internet makes a large amount of information available to anyone who wants to access it. In using a computer or mobile device, you leave behind a large amount of information about yourself. For example, your computer logs your movement through the Internet, storing information in your browser's history. The cached history reveals every webpage you visit. You can erase this information to some extent on your own computer, but if you are connected to a server, the record is maintained, typically without user access. In addition, websites collect a large amount of information from you when you access the site. In general, your device's information and other demographic information are freely available to anyone who chooses to collect it. Information-literate individuals are aware of this reality and take precautions accordingly. Installing and running software designed to detect malware, such as spyware, and other unwanted intrusions is a "must" in today's electronic world.

CRITICAL THINKING QUESTIONS

- Should a "right to be forgotten" law be implemented in the United States? Why or why not?
- Should the personal rights of individuals be sacrificed for the public right to security? Why or why not?
- How can you protect the personal information stored on your computer and mobile devices?

INFORMATION AND SECURITY ISSUES

In addition to understanding and abiding by the legal and ethical uses of information, information-literate people follow the recommended security precautions associated with receiving, viewing, and transmitting content and materials. They are also aware of the following common security issues facing information users.

COMPUTER SECURITY

Because much of what professionals do with information takes place on a computer and the Internet, these systems must be kept as secure as possible. This is true regardless if the computer is a desktop PC, laptop, tablet, smartphone, or other mobile device. Maintaining security and following security guidelines help to ensure that the information received and sent is free of harmful software and does not infringe upon others' privacy or copyright.

Some guidelines for computer system security are the following:

- **Maintain current security protection on your computer.** Protecting your computer and the network alike from incoming viruses, worms, spyware, and other destructive software programs is vital to your privacy and safety, and that of others. Security is achieved by installing and continually renewing security software, keeping operating systems updated with the latest security patches, and staying current on the latest security issues related to computers and the Internet. Many operating systems and security programs will even include features that allow you to automatically download and install updates on a scheduled basis. In addition, both spyware and virus programs can be configured to check your system for problems regularly.
- **Practice safe emailing procedures.** Email can bring viruses and other destructive software programs to your computer and smart devices, especially in attached files. Never open an attachment in an email if you are not sure who sent it to you, or if it looks suspicious in any way. Hackers can send destructive programs through other people's email addresses—even people you know. If you are not expecting to receive an email with an attachment from a friend, classmate, or colleague, confirm that this person indeed sent it to you before you open it.
- **Protect your computer when using wireless technology.** Many users of mobile devices access the Internet via wireless technology. You must secure your system to protect yourself from hackers who tap into wireless networks in an attempt to access or read information, email, and other types of correspondence. This is especially easy to do in a public-access wireless hotspot, such as a coffee shop, hotel, or airport. Hackers can access shared files and read anything on a computer. They also can see the information being transmitted over the Internet. For example, if you are using an unsecured wireless access

point in a coffee shop to make a banking transaction and a hacker is sitting at the table next to you, you may be giving up your passwords, account numbers, and other confidential information.

- **Practice safe and ethical networking.** Never access an account except the one assigned to you. Also, never access another person's folders or files without his or her permission.
- **Do not use your work's computer resources for personal activities.** This policy often is enforced in businesses and schools. Whatever you do on an organization's computer system can be viewed and retrieved by system administrators, even if you have deleted the material.
- **Never send or make available obscene, vulgar, rude, derogatory, discriminatory, or slanderous materials on a computer or smart device.** This practice is potentially illegal, as well as highly unethical and unprofessional. In addition, you should be wise not to send or distribute unsolicited email, also known as spam, even if it is cute, humorous, informative, touching, or harmless. Spam takes up a lot of time and server space and has no place in a work setting.
- **Do not violate copyright laws.** This means that you should neither send copyrighted material to others nor make it available on a network without receiving the appropriate permission to do so. The exception is when the use falls within the fair-use guidelines for certain research and educational activities.
- **Do not violate privacy laws.** If you were to access or make available the private information of others, you would be violating privacy laws. This also means that you should never transmit audio or video clips of others or publish individuals' pictures without their written permission.
- **Use secure passwords.** Passwords and PINs help to secure network and computer access, as well as access to individual folders and files. Be smart about your password selection. Passwords should be difficult to guess. For example, a password consisting of your son's name and birthday may be easily compromised. A password consisting of random letters and

6

numbers, such as ffg62thk, is a better choice. Although random passwords are more difficult to remember, they are much more secure. Also, select passwords with both numbers and letters to increase the difficulty of guessing. In most systems (though not all), special characters (e.g., $, %, &) can be used to increase the level of difficulty. Change passwords regularly and at any time you think someone has gained access to them. Never leave your password list on your computer or in an area in which it can be easily retrieved.

- **Back up your files.** Even the most diligent, safety-conscious computer or mobile device users are susceptible to a crash or other major malfunction. Electronic equipment eventually breaks down. To ensure that a crash or virus does not become a crisis for you, back up your important electronic files in a safe manner, and store the backup files in a different and secure location. You can back up files using flash drives or external hard drives; however, these types of storage solutions are susceptible to damage and may not last as long as you need the files. Data backup software is inexpensive (and, in some cases, free) and is a more reliable option. You also can make use of cloud-based storage from third-party vendors that allow you to upload and store your files on their servers. Be sure to check the credibility of the vendor, though.

  Whatever method you use, store your backup files in a location different from that of your computer or network so if some disaster strikes your building, both your computer and your backups will not be there. For extremely important documents, consider making a hard copy of the file and storing it in a safe place.

  Be sure to back up your files often when you are working on a document, and save the drafts of your work as separate files. This procedure will protect you in case your file becomes infected with a virus, corrupted, or degraded in some way. It could also play an important role in proving that the work is yours in the event that someone steals (plagiarizes) the material.

- **Be aware of Internet scams.** Internet scams consist of any activity in which someone tries to sell you products fraudulently, gain personal information from you, or get you to invest in some illegal or nonexistent project. Common

6

SELF-ASSESSMENT QUESTIONS

- How secure is your own computer system and the network you use daily?
- How secure are your mobile devices?
- What specific security steps do you take currently?
- How could you improve your security?
- What security steps or policies are taken at your school? (You may have to do some research.) Are these adequate? Do you feel protected?
- Can you think of any policies you would recommend to your school?

Internet scams include illegal online auctions, money offers, work-at-home plans, get-rich-quick schemes, travel and vacation offers, and prizes and sweepstakes. Some of these activities are called "phishing" expeditions, with the goal of getting your money, personal information (e.g., social security number or credit card numbers), and other private data such as usernames and passwords. An example is the unsolicited email that makes an offer and requests your credit card number in return.

PUT IT TO USE Go to http://www.consumer.ftc.gov/scam-alerts to view a list of their most recent scam alerts. This government website helps to keep the American public informed about fraudulent activities, many of which involve sophisticated technologies. This site is updated on a regular basis.

Critical Thinking Question

- How might a lack of security in regard to those with whom you work impact you personally? List as many ways as you can.

6

CASE IN POINT: IT'S NOT WHAT YOU KNOW BUT WHO YOU KNOW

Lily Scala recently graduated from a school in North Carolina as a computer science major. Her first job is working at a software company that specializes in accounting and finance. In her daily interactions with clients Lily hears various accounting and finance terms with which she is not familiar, and she finds it frustrating that she does not know the language. Because of this, she finds it difficult to interact with her clients.

Lily was offered initial training when she first started her job, but much of it was through human resources and not specific to her job description. When she needs to provide information to her clients she often does a Google search but finds that many times Google only provides general information and nothing that is specific to her organization.

- Aside from a Google search, what are some other ways that Lily can find the information she needs to do her job and help her clients?
- What types of resources might Lily use to help her understand the industry in which she works?

THE IMPORTANCE OF INFORMATION LITERACY IN THE WORKPLACE

As you have learned, information literacy is comprised of many components. These include:

- critical thinking, creative thinking, problem solving, and higher-order thinking.
- effective communication and organizational skills.
- computer, library, media, visual, and technology literacy.

As an information worker, you are called on to use all of these components in some fashion and to some degree to solve information problems.

Self-Assessment Questions

- Using the listed components of information literacy, in what areas do you feel you are the strongest?
- What might you do to strengthen the areas that you have identified as being weak points?

Transitioning to the workplace will require you to use these skills in a variety of combinations and in ways that you might not have imagined. As stated earlier, the way you use information in school supports your own learning goals. In the workplace, however, the information environment supports the goals of the organization. Here is your opportunity to show your employer that you are an information-literate employee by positively contributing to the company's goals through your use of your literacy skills to solve information problems.

WHAT EMPLOYERS SEEK

Employers have certain expectations of their new hires, especially recent graduates. While they are looking for technical skills that apply directly to the job and the organization, they also seek fundamental and foundational skills in their employees that can be applied across all industries and job titles.

In a 2012 study by the group Project Information Literacy (projectinfolit.org), employers were asked to identify their expectations and provide an assessment of their new college hires' ability to solve information problems. The following list addresses the competencies that employers seek but recent college hires seldom demonstrate:

- **Asking others on the team to help with research**. Employers found that recent hires tended to conduct research on their own, much as they did in college, as opposed to turning to others in the organization to help them solve information problems. Employers further commented that new hires failed to grasp the importance of collaboration with others as a way to research answers and solve problems. Workplace research is considered interdependent and structured, thus observed organizational behaviors are as important, if not more important, than mere facts and figures. As you learned in the Introduction to Information Literacy chapter, effective communication takes place when the standards of a specific discourse community are considered and information is communicated according to those standards. Now that you are familiar with the communication process and the role of discourse community standards, you are well positioned to meet the collaborative research requirements of the modern workplace.

- **Going beyond a cursory Google search**. This competency speaks directly to finding information beyond what is available online. College students tend to do all of their research online and consider that sufficient. In the workplace, employers expect that new hires will go beyond the computer and seek answers using nondigitized materials such as company reports, manuals, books, and most importantly, human capital. New hires often do not consider their colleagues as valuable sources of information, and yet those very people have organizational experience and knowledge that goes well beyond what the new hire has learned to date. In the How Do You Find and Access Information chapter, you received an introduction to a myriad of information sources. Although each of them is valuable, school librarians were singled out as being particularly important due to the wealth of expertise they possess. If you take the initiative to solicit the feedback of your librarian, your ability to evaluate information will improve and you will be better prepared to interact and learn from future colleagues.
- **Fitting pieces of the information puzzle together**. This involves higher-order thinking. Recall Bloom's Taxonomy from the Introduction to Information Literacy chapter. Thinking involves six levels: knowledge (lowest), comprehension, application, analysis, synthesis, and evaluation (highest). Employers noted that college hires often failed to properly analyze,

synthesize, or evaluate information and to find correlations and patterns among information bits, or to be able to find the value in or the importance of those bits of information. Your new-found understanding of the third and fourth steps in the research process, which involve the critical analysis, evaluation, and organization of information, will be particularly valuable in terms of meeting this workplace competency.

- **Adopting a wide-ranging research approach to finding information.** College students, while conducting research online (and only using online sources), tend to search for information as quickly as possible and assume that the first (or second or third) informational nugget that they find is the best. In the workplace, employers need employees who can conduct a comprehensive search for information using myriad sources, and then use critical and creative thinking skills to solve information problems on behalf of the organization (Head, 2012). The Introduction to Information Literacy chapter discusses a six step problem-solving process that can be utilized in the workplace. As an information-literate individual, you are now able to use these steps to define a problem, identify its real causes, develop and evaluate solution alternatives, implement the best solution, and evaluate the results.

WHAT GRADUATES BRING

The same Project Information Literacy (2012) study also queried recent college graduates about the differences between conducting research to complete college work and using information to solve information problems in the workplace. Not surprisingly, these new hires relied on their tried-and-true way of conducting online research but struggled with the transition between school and work.

When interviewed, participants noted three major challenges in transitioning from college to the workplace. All three challenges related to their abilities to solve information problems in the workplace based upon the skills and strategies they learned while conducting course-related research in school. These challenges include the following:

- **Embracing a "get it done now" attitude.** New college hires struggled with the immediacy of needing to find and communicate information. Gone were the days of having an entire semester to work on a project, when and where they wanted. Participants said this sense of urgency left them with feelings of vulnerability, being replaceable, and being constantly hurried.
- **No clear sense of direction is given.** Despite some initial training when they were hired, participants said that this formal training was not ongoing and that change was constant within the organization. With less direction on how to solve information problems in the workplace, those interviewed expressed feelings of disorientation and fear.
- **Finding information must be done within the framework of the organization and its people.** Conducting research while in college is typically not considered a social activity. Even if you work on a project as part of a team, the chances are great that you are still finding and evaluating the information you need on your own and bringing it back to the larger group. That is generally not the case in the workplace, however. Colleagues, supervisors, and trusted coworkers can all have the information you are seeking when a quick Google search cannot yield the answer. Participants noted that using traditional forms of research, such as seeking the expertise of colleagues, was a remarkably efficient and productive way of solving information problems in the workplace (Head, 2012).

Digital Vision/Getty Images

Critical Thinking Question

- Do you think that finding and using information is social? Why or why not?

6

STRATEGIES FOR BEING A PROFESSIONAL INFORMATION WORKER

So how do you go about transitioning how you find and evaluate information from the classroom to the workplace? Research suggests that early on in their careers college graduates must modify how they operate as an information worker to fit into the "information culture" of their organization (Head, 2012). This, coupled with entering a fast-paced workplace, makes doing information work seem challenging, if not daunting. Head (2012) offers some strategies that can be employed to help you make that transition as suggested by interviews with recent graduates in the Project Information Literacy study.

- **Use your supervisor as an information source to build knowledge.** Your supervisor is privy to organizational decisions that you are likely not as a new employee, and he or she understands why those decisions are being made. He or she is fully entrenched in the "information culture" of your organization and thus becomes a valuable and valued resource.
- **Seek out relationships with trusted coworkers.** While it may be quickest and easiest to seek out information from your supervisor, oftentimes coworkers can be a reliable source of information. These people may or may not be a part of your immediate team. Take the time to get to know others in the organization that can provide you with guidance and make a point of learning from them.
- **Go online first, and then ask a coworker for additional information.** As a recent graduate, your first reaction to solving an information problem may be to look online. Generally, there is nothing wrong to this approach, but online sources may not give you the answers you are seeking. Google and other search engines do not know the ins and outs of your organization and thus cannot provide you with the contextualized information that you need. If searching online can give you background information on a topic, it is a valid approach. Take that information to a coworker and ask for help in filling in the gaps to solve the information problem that is unique to your organization.
- **Use networked knowledge and Internet sources to find experts.** This is an especially helpful approach if the information problem you are solving is very technical in nature. Online forums can help you find the information that you need if you cannot get the answers from someone at work.

Clearly there is no single "best" way to solve information problems in the workplace. Your most successful strategy for doing so will be your ability to build your own professional "social network" comprised of your supervisor, trusted coworkers, and outside experts who can guide you in completing your daily tasks. In this way, you will become a professional information worker.

Self-Assessment Questions

- How comfortable are you seeking out information from relative strangers in the workplace?
- What strategies might you employ to gain confidence in speaking to those whom you do not know at work?

Critical Thinking Question

- What are some strategies you might use to help build your "social network" at work?

CHAPTER SUMMARY

In this chapter, you learned about the importance of using information legally and ethically and how to communicate it effectively to others. This includes the concepts of intellectual property, copyright, plagiarism, and fair use. You also learned about the need to properly cite and document the sources of information in your materials. Of additional concern is how information and privacy issues interact, as well as information privacy and security issues. You learned about aspects of communicating information so it is understood and used in the most legal, ethical, and effective ways. Finally, you learned about the information literacy skills you should learn while in school, the importance of being information-literate in the workplace, and strategies for being a professional information worker.

POINTS TO KEEP IN MIND

In this chapter, several main points were discussed in detail:

- Intellectual property refers to anything created by the mind, such as literary works, artwork, inventions, logos or symbols, names, designs, images or photographs, and other types of multimedia.
- Copyright reflects the rights given to creators of some forms of expressions of intellectual property. Copyrights are protected by copyright laws.
- Plagiarism and cyber plagiarism are unethical and illegal practices. They are a growing problem in educational and professional settings.
- Style guides are used to properly cite information sources. Standard style guides, among others, include the APA Style, the MLA Style, and the Chicago Style.
- Privacy related to information literacy means that individuals using information should maintain the privacy of other individuals' personal information.
- Securing information on a computer or mobile device is an increasingly important topic. Guidelines for how to protect information housed on a computer aid in protecting that information.

- Employers seek recently graduated new hires with a wide variety of information literacy skills.
- Preparing to become a professional information worker will support your success in the workplace.

apply it

Activity #1: Personal Note-taking Procedure

GOAL: To develop a personal note-taking procedure that avoids plagiarism when conducting research.

STEP 1: Think carefully about how you can take notes during the research process. Develop a plan of action for your note-taking procedure to help you formalize how you take notes.

STEP 2: Write this plan in a step-by-step procedure format, and place your plan in your portfolio. If you find it useful, create a checklist that will help you follow the plan during any research activity.

Activity #2: Computer Security Evaluation

GOAL: To emphasize the importance of computer security and to evaluate the current level of your computer's security.

6

STEP 1: Develop a checklist for your computer security. Include all relevant steps, programs, and procedures to ensure safe computing in your personal home office and workspace, as well as in your workplace.

STEP 2: Use your checklist to evaluate the security level of your current situation.

STEP 3: Develop a plan to optimize your security situation in any place where you use your computer.

Activity #3: Citation Exploration

GOAL: To demonstrate an understanding of how to cite information sources properly.

STEP 1: Determine the acceptable style used in your institution or workplace for citing information sources.

STEP 2: Search for information on using this style.

STEP 3: Acquire the official style guide and implement use of this style in each assignment, research task, and other written document.

SUGGESTED ITEMS FOR LEARNING PORTFOLIO

Refer to the "How to Use This Book" section at the beginning of this textbook for more information on learning portfolios.

- Personal Note-taking Plan
- Computer Security Evaluation Checklist

REFERENCES

The Chicago Manual of Style. 16th ed. (2010). Chicago: University of Chicago Press.

Head, A. (2012). *Learning Curve: How College Graduates Solve Information Problems Once They Join the Workplace.* Retrieved February 6, 2016, from http://projectinfolit.org/images/pdfs/pil_fall2012_workplacestudy_fullreport_revised.pdf

Manjoo, F. (2015). *'Right to Be Forgotten' Online Could Spread.* Retrieved February 1, 2016, from http://www.nytimes.com/2015/08/06/technology/personaltech/right-to-be-forgotten-online-is-poised-to-spread.html?_r=0

Mears, B. (2014). *Supreme Court: Police Need Warrant to Search Cell Phones.* Retrieved February 5, 2016, from http://www.cnn.com/2014/06/25/justice/supreme-court-cell-phones/

MLA Handbook. 8th ed. (2016). New York: Modern Language Association of America.

Patry, W. F. (1994, 2000). *Copyright Law and Practice.* Retrieved June 18, 2013, from http://digital-law-online.info/patry/patry5.html

Publication Manual of the American Psychological Association. 6th ed. (2010). Washington, DC: American Psychological Association.

United States Code. (2014). *Copyright Law of the United States of America and Related Laws Contained in Title 17 of the United States Code*. Retrieved March 13, 2016, from http://www.copyright.gov/title17/

United States Copyright Office. (2016). *eCO Registration System.* Retrieved February 8, 2016, from http://copyright.gov

University System of Georgia Board of Regents. (n.d. [a]). *Giving Credit Where Credit is Due.* Retrieved June 18, 2013, from http://www.usg.edu/galileo/skills/unit08/credit08_09.phtml

University System of Georgia Board of Regents. (n.d. [b]). *Public Domain.* Retrieved June 18, 2013, from http://www.usg.edu/galileo/skills/unit08/credit08_10.phtml

6

Index

B

C

F

G

H

I